Manifesting Excellence

By Myechia Barnett

The Abundance Builder, LLC

Published by Barnett Publishing

Introduction

Are you going through something right now and you need a little encouragement or push? Have you noticed what manifested in your life, even if it does not look like it? Maybe you have manifested something in your life, and you had to undergo the challenges of life until it did manifest? God will do that sometimes right? Read about the lives of these amazing women who share a piece of themselves by breaking down how God brought them through some tough times. What they wanted happened for them because they did NOT give up. God MANIFESTED it into their lives. Are you ready to take a trip on this amazing ride into Manifesting Excellence with us? After reading this book, we hope to bring awareness that God is still in the blessing business and manifestations are happening. He has not forgotten about YOU. He remembers everything you prayed and ask for; just be patient because when He does it for you, it was worth the wait.

Chapter 1

''Winning doesn't always mean being first'' Manifest Your Dream Life!

By Marla Hunter

My name is Marla Hunter; I am a 24-year-old mother & business owner. I wear many hats & with wearing many hats comes many titles. My titles are: Mother, CEO, Business Owner, Cook, Menstrual Hygiene Coach, Brand Ambassador, Financial Advisor/Financial

Investor/Digital Entrepreneur & last but not least, a Co-Author! Having several businesses can be overwhelming of course; however, it is also life-changing and amazing. I am so grateful for all the success I have endured since I started my journey of Entrepreneurship. I say if there is anything in this world that you are passionate about and love, GO FOR IT! Life waits for no one and if you just sit around waiting for the "perfect moment" to do something, you will never do it. Anything in life can be yours if you BELIEVE IT CAN BE! You see, belief is an acceptance that a statement is true or something that exists. My chapter is called ''Manifest Your Dream Life.'' I chose this for the title of my chapter because I just want to share with you all how I manifested my Dream life & still am. We all have dreams; we dream of what we want to do and be when we were kids. Some of us execute those dreams, and some don't or just never have the chance to. There are so many things I dream of having and doing and I am manifesting those dreams one day at a time. Are you aware of what manifestation is or means? If you don't know what it means, then I strongly encourage you to take some time out of your day and research it. Do you know you are in control of your own destiny? ''You are the creator of your universe. Breathe life into your legacy''- A wise woman once told me. Those words make me feel so powerful & I hope sharing them with you all makes you feel powerful too! We have to understand that in life, you are bound to have distractions, but that doesn't mean you have to be distracted. WHEN YOU WANT TO HAVE SUCCESS AS BAD AS YOU WANT TO BREATHE, YOU ARE GOING TO BE SUCCESSFUL.

Your mindset is what is going to determine your success. Discipling yourself, motivating yourself, staying focused, dedicated and determined, you can manifest ANYTHING you want. I have been an Entrepreneur and Business Owner for over a year now. It feels so amazing to say that. I have found my purpose! My career. My life mission is to impact lives, educate, save wombs, and help women, men and kids to regain their confidence. I am the CEO of Diamond Luxuries, my brand, which is also my PASSION and LIFE PURPOSE! I am so excited to walk you guys through my journey of manifestation. Here's a fun fact about me being a ''Co-Author'' in this book; believe it or not, I MANIFESTED that. I have always wanted to be in a book or write a book since I was young. I have been wanting to write a book for the longest, but I didn't know where to start. Just this past year, I said to myself ''I want to write a book,' and then, this amazing opportunity came to me. I felt as though it was one of those opportunities that I have been praying to God about and asking Him for so long & it finally happened, so I jumped at it. Sometimes we delay our own blessings. What I mean by this is that we can constantly pray to God and ask Him for things; however, He isn't just going to give you what you are asking for overnight. You have to realize that He is going to send obstacles and challenges your way to see if you are ready and prepared for the blessings you are asking for. Understand that these hurdles and obstacles you are facing is not the end of your story; it is only the beginning. The positive of obstacles is that every obstacle has an opportunity. You have the ability to overcome obstacles; you are the only thing standing in your way. When we better ourselves, we attract better. These things are prepping you into the person you are destined to be. I'm always so grateful because one thing about God is that He always answers your prayers. Taking care of people and helping them is something I love doing and I am beyond ecstatic that I created businesses where I am able to do that. Uplifting, making a difference, empowering, encouraging and being there for someone is all that matters to me.

www.diamondluxuries.site

Chapter 2

Growth and Development

By: Quila Harvey

My favorite quote is "Keep Moving Forward"

Walt Disney

Whew, Chile! Where do I begin? Oh, hey, I am Quila Harvey well Osborne is my maiden name. I was married and got a divorce a few years ago. I kept the last name because I thought it would be too much to hassle to change with the bank, bills, etc. Anyway, speaking of all that, I was in a bad marriage, and I was trying to build my business during that marriage. I am a mother of 6, so it was hard to juggle the kids' work, cook, clean, run a business, and have someone mentally trying to bring you down. A lot of us have been through it, unfortunately.

Let's go back a bit.

I was born in South Bend, IN raised in Atlanta, GA. I've always been the ambitious type, never afraid to do anything at all. My personality was always outgoing and fun. I was very popular in school. I wasn't the brightest kid at all, but I managed lol. Actually, I was quite the roughneck, climbing trees playing ball, etc. Who would ever think I would end up with 6 children? Yes honey, 6 of them and they all are awesome. Growing up, I had a great life; my father always kept us in the latest fashion. My mother was married to a guy in the music industry, so I was able to meet some folks and go to a few concerts. I had a very fun life which led up to me becoming a rapper. Lady Que is what I called myself, which is also my podcast name. I was pretty damn dope if I do say so myself. I think making music was one of my greatest moments. Meeting celebs being in the limelight parties at mansions, all that.

That lifestyle allowed me to follow my dreams. That was really my first love, and I was able to do it and not be afraid. At that time, I was a mother of 1 child, my son, who is now 17. I had him everywhere with me, studios and video shoots. At the age of 3, my son met a lot of cool artists that are famous now. I am "like hey son," pointing at the man on TV "you met that guy before." He would be like, "dang mom, why aren't you still rapping lol." Doing music was so awesome but I had to stop because I ended up having my second child; he wasn't planned at all. At that point, I was ready to give up on life.

I was so stressed out I attempted suicide because the sperm donor wasn't supportive, and I didn't want to keep my baby. I ended up keeping him, ended up working a regular job and had limited fun because my mother didn't want to babysit. I was depressed for a while because I felt I missed out on a lot of things in my life. Fast forward, I ended up in Indianapolis, IN. I can't stand Indianapolis lol. That's where things became bittersweet. Let me tell you why, first off, I thought I met a great guy, things happened so fast. We had 5 kids back-to-back; one of them passed away, which is who I named my business 'The Beautiful By Bri'nae' after.

I started The Beautiful By Bri'nae in 2013. First, I started selling hair, clothing then I decided to sell everything else under the sun. My husband at the time was halfway supportive. So, I started working in the pharmacy field, running my brand being a mom and a wife all at once. Although I was married, he didn't help me at all with the kids; he figured if he paid bills, he could do as he pleases and not help me at all. Then my father passed away, which caused a lot of issues. I started being abused emotionally and physically, I was called names; I was told I wasn't going to be successful. I was lied to, cheated on and all that. I was at another point of letting go again. I felt so drained but one thing about me is I never give up. Working in the pharmacy, I became infatuated with skin and products. My mother was a dermatologist nurse assistant growing up. I always had a thing for skincare. So, I started my own skincare brand. I also told myself I was going to become an Esthetician.

Me and my ex-husband divorced but there was still a living situation where the kids and I were living with him due to me not having family close and court issues. I never gave up, I ran my skincare brand and I started doing things for myself mentally to ignore the things going on. Although the physical abuse stopped, he kept mentally trying to bring me down. I started reading, I started soul searching, doing things with my kids, meditating, doing moon rituals, praying and all that. I told myself Que, keep moving forward; you got this, and I kept going. I wrote down things I wanted to manifest like becoming an Esthetician and having a successful skincare line. I started seeing my angel numbers more and more. I never gave up being called ugly, being told my little business wasn't going to make it.

I blocked him out; I took every little piece of name-calling and harsh bashing and got into school, got my certificate and became a licensed Esthetician. Why because I didn't give up, I manifested my excellence and my dreams, and I made it happen.

That's what you have to do, you have to grow and develop yourself because no one is going to do that shit for you. Oh, and believe me, when it gets rough, you might feel like saying fuck it sometimes. Don't stop keep moving forward, as Walt Disney said.

Things will get better for you if you keep going, I promise. No matter who says what, you have the power to manifest anything, and God will put you where you need to be. I hope this brings the greatness out of someone because I have been through it and I want everyone who is going through it regardless of the living situation because it is hard at times; trust me, I'm telling you to not give up.

The Beautiful by Bri'nae

www.brinae.shop

Chapter 3

"Impossible and Improbable, but I still did it!"-Dr. McGill

By Dr. Michelle McGill Murph

Many times, we are swept up in the roaring tides of life. We shoulder many responsibilities; we are parents, siblings, sons/daughters, spouses, and everything else in between. We rarely take time to reflect or remain mindful, especially when we are barely surviving. Our hopes, dreams, and aspiration can feel just like that, just hopes and dreams. Nelson Mandela said, "It always seems impossible until it is done." As I reflect on my life to date, this quote resonates most. It may have been impossible, but I still did it!

Allow me to introduce myself; I am Dr. Michelle McGill. A chiropractor, certified medical examiner, wife, and mother. Despite my accomplishments at heart, I am a girl that turned stumbling blocks into steppingstones; and was able to achieve the seemingly impossible. By truly embracing the promise God has over my life. When my world didn't reflect the promise, I used mind of matter; to push, pivot, climb and manifest excellence. Maybe you need a breakthrough, hope, confidence, a change in circumstances, healing, comfort, provision, or restoration. God is big enough to trust, no matter the size of the problem. The only thing that is standing between you and your goals is YOU! I want to encourage you to adjust your perspective because life is too long to live unhappy or unfulfilled.

I was born and raised in Brooklyn, New York. More specifically, I grew up in the East New York section of Brooklyn. The East New York section sits in the shadow of John F. Kennedy Airport, easily accessed from The Belt Parkway, The Jackie Robinson Parkway, The Conduit, and Route 27, better known as Linden Boulevard. East New York is a place of irony, a place that was accessible yet cut off. A place of chaos and a place of solace. East New York was the place of failing schools yet produced thriving scholars. East New York was a place of stagnation and of growth. East New York was home of high crime and corruption; it was literally a dumping ground. East New York's unique positions can be attributed to gentrification. With all East New York was, there is no other place that I would rather have spent my formative years. Navigating the streets of Brooklyn made me resilient; it made me bold.

As a very young child, I had many dreams, but the dream that stands out most is my dream of being an archeologist. I would sit looking through books and imagine how I was the one to make the discoveries documented on the pages. However, there was this one thing, when God made me, He did not add a dash of "a love for all things nature." And growing up in the concrete jungle of New York City was not changing my mind. As I reflect, I really wanted to be an archeologist more so because it was a big word that I knew how to say; it was different, it was a head-turner, and I was fascinated by the Egyptian culture. I am still fascinated by ancient Egyptian's civilization and its many influences on modern-day society. Egyptians invented mathematics, geometry, surveying, metallurgy, astronomy, accounting, writing, paper, medicine. They invented the ramp, the lever, the plough, mills for grinding grain, and pretty much all the makings that go into large, organized societies. When asked "what do you want to be when you grow up?" Me stating, "I wanted to be an archeologist;" was a proclamation. Each time I was proclaiming and embracing that I can control my narrative. I didn't have to accept the boxes anyone want to put me in. I didn't have to accept the cliché doctor, lawyer, or president of the United States. So how did I end up in health care? It was not long after I recognized the significance and work that goes into such positions making worthy proclamations. Archeologist was catchy but nothing is more eye-catching than the ways God will show up in your life. God will allow things in your life to help you discover your path, hone the tools you will need along the journey. When God proclaims there is no ambiguity, it will be known it was divine.

I am the eldest of my three siblings. My younger brother was born with a dysfunctional liver. Simply put, the liver is responsible for filtering and removing toxins from our blood.

My brother's non-functional liver equaled numerous complications, including seizures and life-threating infections like sepsis. My brother had a team of doctors working to keep him alive. There were surgeries and hospital stays from the complications. My brother only had one chance at survival. His only chance was a liver transplant.

Transplants are complicated procedure, even with the many advances we made to date. Each successful transplant should be celebrated for the miracle it is. But to bring context to the time, this was in the early 80s. The first liver transplant was performed in 1963 on a pediatric patient and was unsuccessful due to uncontrollable bleeding. The surgery was attempted by various surgeons and remained unsuccessful until 1967. Throughout, the 1970s liver transplants remained experimental as viable techniques were developed. Even if the surgery was successful, there was only one-year survival rate of 25% due to numerous complications from rejection and infection. The prognosis was bleak but there were no other options. This was the treatment my brother needed his only chance.

With no other options, my parents placed my brother on the organ donor list and were given a beeper. "The Beeper," as we referred to it, was my brother's last hope, a lifeline. It sat in our living room on top of the TV; it was kept central in our apartment so that anyone would be able to hear it if it went off. There were countless times "The Beeper" went off; there were so many false alarms over the years. It was October of 1990 that "The Beeper" went off and it wasn't a false alarm; it was in the middle of the night. A crisp fall night in New York City, my mother packed my sister and I into the car and took us to my grandmother's house. It was on this night that God answered a prayer. My father is a simple man and he was a man that never felt to ask God for anything else. When I was in my 20s, I finally asked my father why and he shared with me an encounter he had days prior to my brother's transplant surgery. My brother's health had deteriorated so much that it had become cruel and selfish to wish life on him or ask him to hold on. My father told me that after four long years, he made peace with the thought of saying goodbye to his child, his only son. He shared that he called to God and pleaded for him to take my brother because he didn't want my brother to suffer anymore. The moment he finished uttering his plea, a white light appeared to him. From that light, he heard a voice clearly tell him not to fear and not to worry anymore; it will be alright. What happened next was nothing short of a miracle. My brother's condition began to improve; he became stable. The fevers normalized, the seizures stopped and then "The Beeper" went off.

My brother had a match, and his transplant took place. His transplant took 32 hours and was successful. In Psalm 50 verse 15, God says, "call me when trouble comes. I will help you and you will honor me." It was in my father's surrender that God was able to breathe life back into my brother and my family.

God's hands were over my brother long before his transplant surgery. As I mentioned previously, my brother's life-saving transplant was risky and came with an unfavorable prognosis, even if it was successful. It was four years before he could get his transplant; if my brother had matched and received his transplant at the immediate recommendation, his chance of long-term survival was slim to none. With the knowledge I have now in hindsight, during our time in the valley, God was not dormant but truly orchestrating a masterpiece, a miracle. While we were in the valley, God was working through many to perfect the surgical technique as well as allow the discovery of the medicines that would be needed for him to survive and combat rejection. It turns out the missing piece of the puzzle was Cyclosporine. Cyclosporine, in the clinical setting used as an immunosuppressant. Cyclosporine is derived from fungi. It was first discovered in soil samples in 1971. Its immunosuppressive effect was discovered the same year. However, the chemical structure was not determined until 1976. Cyclosporine was not approved for use until 1983 in adult patients. Cyclosporine is a powerful drug that can have adverse consequences, including kidney and liver failure. When my brother had his procedure, it was still considered experimental and came with many unknowns. But God was the footprints in the sand, and I am happy to share my brother has and continues to live a full life.

This experience had a profound impact on my life, both positive and negative. It was during this time I discovered my love for healthcare and even if it were cliché, I wanted to also be an agent of healing. I decided I would one day become a doctor. I developed my independence and ability to teach myself; I became self-reliant. Although, it was never directly asked of me, seeing my parents go through such a heartache sparked a desire to do all I could to support the people I love. Everything my parents had was diverted into keeping this child alive. With my brother's grave prognosis carried an unimaginable heaviness. To no fault of theirs, there were times my parents just weren't available, leaving me vulnerable to the world with a deep feeling of loneness. Would this be my understanding if I were older? I am sure it wouldn't have been. But, as a young child, it was no other way that I could comprehend it; other than "I am on my own and I have to take care of myself."

My independence and self-reliance are now my greatest strength but at one time, it was a weakness. Just as you can manifest excellence, you can also manifest chaos. I had a deep sense of loneness. When coupled with trauma, I began to question if God was real or if it was just science. I had cast aside the stories I was told. This false narrative became so intense, and it was consuming. I lost interest in everything! I no longer wanted to play sports; I no longer wanted to go to school, I no longer had dreams; I no longer had the will to live. I was so numb nothing mattered. That was until a few months before my 16th birthday; I gave birth to a baby boy. I knew nothing about being a mother. The moment my water broke, my whole life changed. I thank God that I was home with my parents at the time because to be honest, I had no idea of what to do. My son came so fast; there was no time to get to the hospital. I delivered him right there in the house surrounded by my family, and at that moment, I realized I was not alone. They assured me that they were there and would be there. As I rode in the ambulance to the hospital with my newborn, there was a renewal. As my son stared at me, I made him a promise that I wouldn't let anything happen to him and that I would not allow us to become a statistic. Recognizing the gravity of his entry into my life and all that he would give me, I named my son Matthew derived from the Hebrew name meaning "gift of God."

Being a teenage mother had its many challenges. Nonetheless, I persevered. It was the toughness I learned in Brooklyn that allowed me to punch all the limitations that many tried to place on I the throat. Every can't was made into a can; my dream of becoming a doctor was renewed. I finished High School with honors and college credit ahead of schedule. I earned a full academic scholarship to Claflin University, where I majored in biochemistry. Again, I excelled in my studies. What I admire most about Claflin is that it was a place with a rich legacy of applying pressure to create diamonds since its inception.

It was in my senior year at Claflin that I was introduced to Chiropractic. Chiropractic derived from Greek words cheir "hand" and pracktikos" practical" is a system of integrative medicine concerned with the diagnosis, treatment of mechanical disorders in the musculoskeletal system, with an emphasis on the vertebral column which house the central nervous system, hence influencing overall health. It was now that God spoke to me; I prayed that God shows me what I was to do. I wanted to go into health care, I had entry into medical school, but it did not "feel right." With that epiphany, I made the decision to pivot and pursued my studies in Chiropractic.

Early on, I remember how hard it was for me to garner support in my decision, see not everyone will understand your journey. Even my supportive mother couldn't understand why I wouldn't want to go to medical school. I remember the countless conversation throughout my first year of studies, but I stood firmly on what God had called me to do. Although, she didn't say much after that year; it wasn't until I was in practice that she truly understood. Seeing me in action and my patient's gratitude, she understood. I am always humbled by the way God has decided to use me. It leaves me in awe and I never take it for granted. It is divine when someone gets back to their activities of daily living. Whether it's a mother being able to pick up her child, a father being able to play with his child, getting an athlete to championship performance or getting someone to a point where they can walk and get dressed on their own. I never take any of it for granted. I am so thankful that I had the courage to surrender and trust in God's promise and direction. A strength that was birthed out of my motherhood and renewal. So, you see, what was meant to be a stumbling block, God used it as a stepping stone; once I trusted in God.

We all can become swept up in the roaring waters of life at those times; we must rely on our anchors. I share parts of my story in hopes that you will see God will allow certain things into our life to shake and move us; there are things that, at the time, we may not understand. Stay mindful even in the valleys we experience because there are lessons, we could learn no other way. Those circumstances may bring us heartache and even feelings of shame. But it is when we fall to our knees and surrender that we get out of God's way. That is when we get to witness God's absolute best. I encourage you to cast aside what others may think of you. Embrace that you have the right to change your mind, growth can be found even in stillness, and some people are just for a season. Just because you are struggling doesn't mean you are failing. It is my prayer that knowledge of God's love and grace show vividly as you move through the world from this day fourth; that you find happiness deep down within, success in every aspect of your life, serenity in each sunrise, love that never ends, a path that leads to bountiful tomorrows and appreciate all the wonderful and unique things about you. It may seem impossible, but you will do it with God!

www.lifetimelifestyles.com

Chapter 4

Dr. Tonya Blackmon

3 Keys to Manifesting an Excellent Life

One in a Million

Hello, I am Dr. Tonya Blackmon, a Valuable, Marketplace Minister, Wife, Mom, Nana, friend, and businesswoman. Thanks for purchasing this book! In this chapter, I will share the strategies I use to live a dream life, unlock potential, and manifest excellence in my daily life. You did not buy this book just because you feel like adding another book to your collection. I know you have heard the old saying, "nothing just happens." As of this writing, Amazon has 33 million books in its database available for sale. This book anthology is one in a million because it is a compilation of the keys the authors have used to manifest excellence.

You are Valuable!

Dream with me- imagine you are sitting alone with your legs up on a beach shore, you can hear the ocean waves, and you are relaxing. While resting, may I ask you a few questions? Do not answer them verbally; think about your answers. If you only had $250 left in your pocket, and a family member asked you to give it to them, would you give even if you need to pay your bill with the money? Next question, does your best friend/partner/spouse actions toward you often make you feel hurt, but you do not share your feelings with them because of fear? Question three, when Mondays come, do you get a headache because you dread going to work and know that you want to do more with your life?

If you feel this way, I understand. For a long time in my life, I was addicted to helping others, even if it hurt me. Here are my answers to the questions I asked you. I would have given the $250, even if it meant my demise. When others hurt me, I would remain silent and stayed in the relationship with them because I was afraid to be alone or accepted ill-treatment as a natural progression in any relationship. As for my career, I have worked many jobs just for money and not for fulfillment. Truthfully, I was afraid to get out of corporate because a steady paycheck was a sure thing, and I was concerned about starting an unsuccessful business. Why did I do that? Why did I allow fear to stop me? Why did I crave approval from others? When I looked in the mirror, I did not see myself as valuable. When I thought about myself, I did not think I had anything significant to share with others.

Let us go deeper. For over twenty years, I have had the honor of providing one-on-one ministry to women from around the world. And for over a decade, my team and I have helped numerous business owners start and grow successful businesses. Today, I am addicted to listening to and reading about the business stories of businesspeople on YouTube, lol. And when I meet a Christian woman that picks up the pieces after enduring a challenging tragedy, I connect with her on purpose. As a proud nerd, I want to know why some people manifest their dreams and why some do not. Learning how they were able to manifest their dreams after all was lost or when they hit rock bottom is empowering to me.

Key #1 Manifesting excellence- You are Valuable!

First, you have permission to allow any situation or person that harms you to exit for good. Listen, per Oxford online dictionary, to be valuable means "a thing that is of great worth." You are valuable! Shout, "I am valuable!" Own your title right now. Write "I am valuable" with lipstick on your bathroom mirror. Order a new T-shirt with the words "I am Valuable" and take a selfie. Share "I am Valuable" on your social media post with your new selfie picture. The fact that you purchased this book at this time is a testament to the fact that you are valuable. Remember, nothing just happens. From this moment forward, I encourage you to walk as a Valuable Being and Live your life based on decisions that will benefit you and your family.

What do you want?

Have you ever met a person who had a big question mark on the top of their head? When you spoke with them, their favorite color is blue on Monday and it changes to purple on Tuesday. They are in an indecisive cycle. They want to start a new business every day, write a book, leave an abusive relationship, hire a coach, lose weight, and on and on, but for several reasons, they never start. Now that you know and own your value, answer the following question. What do you really want to do with your life – Body, Soul, Spirit, family, career/business, relationship, home, car, etc.? I challenge you-get a clean piece of paper and answer this question. Better yet, make a digital vision board of the answers.

Consequently, for as long as I can remember, I journaled my thoughts, desires, and plans. When I rededicated my life to Jesus Christ, I started recording nightly dreams and notes from prayer. Friend, over twenty years ago in dreams, I saw myself traveling the world, writing books, serving others, and running successful businesses. Today, I am living what I dreamed.

For years in church, people of God were inspired to prophecy successful enterprises over my family and me. After I created my first vision board, I took it to church and prayed over it at the altar. During that time in my life, I was desperate, hurt and confused. My husband and I were on the brink of divorce, and I was worried about how I would provide food for my family and pay the mortgage. Those days are behind us now. My husband and I will be celebrating our 30th anniversary in Hawaii next year. Read on so that I can tell you how I went from a confused mind a with negative bank account to peace and almost $20K (and counting, wink) some months.

Be honest with yourself. Are you living your dream life? What gives you peace? Success is different for each person. Having an abundance of money is not my main concern. Wearing red bottom shoes and having several Birkin bags are not my goals. My success rests in having a meaningful relationship with my family. I just opened two Mother's Day packages and my youngest son just made us homemade pasta for dinner. My family shows me they care about me, which outweighs all the money in the world. Earlier, I suggested that you really consider your family goals because having money and nobody to share it with could/have led to sadness for some people. Money does not take the place of relationships.

Key #2 Manifesting excellence- Develop a Strategic Action Plan

How to Unlock Your Dreams

Vision boards are ineffective if you just look at it. To achieve all the goals on my first vision board, I had to develop an action plan for each goal. Yes, doing this activity will require sacrifice and time. However, in the end, it was worth the investment because all but one of my dreams manifested. For instance, ten years before I earned a doctorate, I printed a degree from google and wrote my name on the degree and pasted it on my board. At the time, I did not know when I was going to achieve my educational goals, but in faith, I knew that it would eventually happen. How long have you been waiting to take a leap of faith? Do you feel that you are too old? Friend, your age or years you have been waiting to start is irrelevant to manifesting your plans. Dust off those dreams, and LEAP NOW!

Key #3 Manifesting excellence- Prayer & Connect with God

Stop! Let us give God all the glory. My family and I are blessed, my God-given potential has been unlocked, and I understand how to manifest excellence in every area of my life. I did not wake up knowing what and how to develop my dreams. It is a journey. Perhaps, you have struggled with knowing your calling and passion. Are they one and the same? Or maybe, you have been gifted in several areas, so you have difficulty in choosing one specific thing? As a woman, I battled with having a successful career and being a good Mom simultaneously. At 18 years old, I joined the military, but I knew that I wanted to be a doctor, so I became a Corpsman. I went to college and prepared for the medical entrance exam, but I could not see myself leaving my young children home for medical school. So, I waited until they were almost grown to pursue a doctoral degree. I have not regretted any choices. Everything manifested for me in divine timing. And it will for you too.

Commit your works to the LORD, and your thoughts will be established (Proverbs 16:3 New King James Version). I love this scripture because it uses the word "thoughts." In other words, when I seek God about my action plans/thoughts, He supernaturally helps them manifest. The key to manifesting ongoing excellence is a combination of prayer and having a connection with God. Here are my secrets. Nobody knows exactly what to do all the time. Nobody is confident every day, all day. Also, perfection does not exist. Friend, if you are waiting on the perfect time to give your action plans feet or waiting on specific connections before launching a new thing, stop and pursue your dreams. Start today where you are. . .

When I was unsure about my calling or purpose, I asked God to show me His will concerning my life. Through dreams and taking the What Color is My Parachute assessment, I got really clear on the direction I wanted for my life. Now, whenever I need clarity, I pray and study the scriptures. If I need physical healing, I find verses on healing and pray it over my life. If I desire more money, I do the same. When I am going through conflicts in relationships, I humble myself, pray and ask God to help me do everything in love. When you get a chance, listen to, or read the book of Nehemiah. Through his story, I learned that fasting, prayer and obeying the voice of God are the key ingredients to manifesting excellence. Nehemiah faced death sentences, ongoing ridicules, and unbelievable circumstances as he pursued his dream of building the wall. Like Nehemiah, let us remember to stay focused and on task when others lie on us, taunt us, and purposely do things to halt our plans. The scripture talks about how the workers held a weapon in one hand while they held a building tool in the other hand as they built the wall. Adversity will come friend but keep building.

Conclusion

According to the online dictionary, excellence is synonymous with "sterling, superlative, great, good, exemplary, exceptional, skillful, admirable, outstanding, magnificent, superb, accomplished, first-rate, attractive, finest, fine, distinguished, exquisite, capital, or champion." And to manifest a thing is to have evidence. When placed together, to manifest excellence means to have accomplished/exceptional evidence of something. In other words, what exceptional fruit is in my life? Your life? My exceptional fruit is extensive because of God. I am married to the man of dreams (Brian). I have three beautiful, talented children (Mike, Bri & BJ), two loving in-laws (Resa & Austin), and four AWESOME, talented grandchildren (Leelee, Millie, Micah, & Cassidy-RIH). My team and I have written winning grants for our clients, and each day we help new people build and finance their business dreams. My health is good, and our bills are paid. God always make sure payroll is paid. When I think about the goals I placed on my vision board several years ago, all but one of them have manifested.

Throughout this chapter, I have shared the three keys I use to manifest excellence in my life.

Key #1 Manifesting excellence- You are Valuable!

Key #2 Manifesting excellence- Develop a Strategic Action Plan

Key #3 Manifesting excellence- Pray & Connect with God

Today, I have new goals, a talented team, my family, and my God. I stand as a woman the Lord has truly blessed. If this chapter has been a blessing to you, or if you decide to walk out manifesting excellence in any area of your life, DM Dr. Tonya on Instagram @onlydrtonyab

Manifesting Excellence Prayer

In Jesus name,

I stand in the gap for every person that reads this book. Jehovah Jireh, your word declares that we have not because we ask not. Humbly, God, I ask that you renew our minds according to your word. Where there is confusion, God gives us clarity. Where there is lack, show us how to manifest prosperity. When innovation is needed, give us new ideas. When balance is needed, tell us what to let go and keep in our daily lives. Teach us how to pray and seek you in all our ways. Remind us to commit our works to you. As we seek your guidance, show us how to manifest our personal, bodily, soul, Spirit, family, career/business, etc. goals. We ask that you make our arms strong for the task at hand and grant us success in our endeavors. We lay every plan, thought, and attack from enemies at your feet. Thank you for allowing us to manifest excellence not only in our personal lives but also in the lives of the people we touch from this moment on. Thank you, Jehovah Jireh!

Amen.

www.drtonyab.com

Chapter 5

Jeniece Drake

NuWave Travel, Inc.

But he said to me, "My grace us sufficient for you, for my power is made perfect in weakness." Therefore, I will boast all the more gladly of my weaknesses, so that the power of Christ may rest upon me. 2 Corinthians 12:9 ESV

Excellence In Weakness

Society conditions us to believe that excellence is the absence of weakness. Those who succeed are superior to those who fail. What they neglect to mention is those who have found success faced failure before attaining their goals. From the day we leave our mother's womb, we begin learning through failure. Not one person walking today fell as a baby and decided, well, I guess walking is not for me. Thomas Edison said, "I have not failed. I've just found 10,000 ways that won't work." When something you try does not turn out as planned, you need to step back, re-evaluate, and adjust to find the right balance to deliver the desired result.

I come from a long line of entrepreneurs, so the boss life is in my blood; the art of the side hustle is strong in my family. When I was in middle school, my parents had to figure out where I got my extra money because I always spent more than I got for allowance. Growing up in New York City Public Housing, my parents took extra precautions to keep my brother and me away from gangs, drugs, and the like, so they were perplexed when they could not figure out where I was getting the extra money. I remember the day my mom confronted me and asked where I was getting the additional funds. I am sure she prepared herself for the worst, but I calmly explained that I was using my allowance to buy candy at the corner store and selling it at a higher price in school. After breathing a sigh of relief that her baby had not turned to a life of crime, she turned to me and said, my God, I raised a hustler. We laugh about it now, but when I think back on these moments, it was evident early in my life that I was born to be great; I just needed proper training.

Knowing that you're destined for something great and holding on to that dream when life hits you is no easy task. People have always pointed out my leadership qualities with special attention to the way my presence often commanded respect, their words not mine. Of course, this was a recipe for disaster that eventually lead to some humbling lessons in life as God prepared me to be the leader He purposed me to be. Pain in our life is not always a signal of God's disapproval or disgust; most times, it is the chastisement and correction of our heavenly Father molding us into what we need to be to fulfill our purpose in life. Whether we realize it or not, our path to perfection in God is hidden in our weaknesses. The areas of my life that felt like hindrances made me lean closer to God. The more life seemed to beat me down, the more I seemed to accomplish! As I hid in the shadow of the Almighty, it became clear that His hand cast that shade while catching everything that life threw at me. Life could shake me, it could knock me down, but it could not claim my life or destiny because the creator and ruler of it all has His hand on me.

When we relinquish our authority to Him, we reclaim our God-given authority over the Earth. We all know the story of Adam & Eve, but we often overlook the fact that they were created and given dominion over the Earth. They relinquished that authority in pursuit of elevating themselves in their might.
When God sent Jesus to redeem us, He reclaimed our birthright; He provided a way back to our position of authority over a world that we are encouraged to fear. The day we give our life back to God, the day we realize we cannot live life without Him, and like the prodigal son return to Him, we begin a training process to become the masters of a realm that has always belonged to us. In our training processes, weakness becomes amplified as the strain of the purge taxes us mentally, physically, and emotionally. The pruning and purging that we all go through may feel like we are being torn apart, but when we endure the process, we emerge whole in His strength.

Most believe that serving God means living life on easy street or that His disciples must be impoverished beggars. In the Bible, there are examples of trials and tribulations that He has helped people rise above. By the time God is done with an enemy of His children, they are left to cower before Him, and because He dwells in you by default, all that oppose your destiny will kneel before you. Earlier I mentioned that my presence commanded authority, something I heard and still hear often. As a young adult, this led to arrogance, but when I got older, I realized it was not me commanding respect in the room; it was God in me. The word of the Lord says that every knee shall bow, and every tongue will confess that He is Lord. If He dwells in us, then those who yield to us are surrendering before the presence and glory of God housed in us. It is not my might or works that cause people to sing my praises. I am nothing more than a beacon of hope, a glimmer of light in a dark world that leads His people back to Him. People often look at others and want what they have without realizing what they had to endure or purge to stand the way they do.

When people look at me, they do not see my struggle; by the grace of God, my family and I have never looked like our circumstances. My circle is small, so most people have no idea that there was a point in my life where my husband and I faced homelessness when our daughter was a toddler. Before my daughter was born, God gave me one last chance to launch my business. I had opened businesses before but always played it safe by giving more effort to the guaranteed paycheck than building the way God told me to. My husband and I came up with a plan that seemed feasible at the time, but man's plans are nothing compared to God's. We planned to stay with family for a year to build our savings and find something that he could handle with a single salary. The goal was to have my business in a position to take care of bills within five years. Of course, none of this went according to plan, and we were in for a fight to manifest what God promised us. It always sounds easy when you are talking it through or writing it down but living it out, well, that is a different story. Financially, we struggled, and we ended up spending more time living with family than anticipated. Staying there became a crutch, we had gotten too comfortable, and God had to shake our foundation to make us move. I come from a close-knit family; we are always there for each other, so when things get turbulent, we re-evaluate the cause of the friction once the dust settles. At the end of the day, it boiled down to God troubling the waters to force us to move so we could continue our journey of growth.

After leaving my family, we struggled to find somewhere to go. I called a friend who is like a sister to me, and she paid for us to stay in a hotel for a few days while we re-grouped. All our options seemed exhausted at the time, and we found ourselves preparing to enter a shelter. I will never forget that night; we still had the hotel room for another day, so we left as much as we could that was of value to avoid any problems traveling to and entering the shelter. We set out to The Bronx from Brooklyn, and as we walked through the area and into the shelter, we stuck out like a sore thumb. I remember realizing I still had my wedding ring on out of habit and turning it backward because it often caught people's attention. We saw parents with their children in broken umbrella strollers while our child sat comfortably in a Graco stroller wrapped warmly in a Bundle Me. My husband and I were standing in line with name-brand coats and clothing, our hearts breaking from what we saw and yet still wondering how we got here. The thoughts that must have been racing through my husband's head at the time were likely maddening. He is our leader, provider, and protector. Yet, all of his promises and intentions had fallen short. How is this what we are facing right now? Despite our circumstance, I was overwhelmed with a desire to have enough to help the people surrounding me. I wanted to provide Accommodate places that would provide them with the dignity and resources they deserved. During my brokenness, pain, desperation, lack, and helplessness, it became abundantly clear that we were living examples that those with relationships with God are covered at a level that hides our shortfalls and struggles. Our rock bottom or glimpse at rock bottom did not look like those who live life without the Father.

When it came time to sit with someone to discuss our situation and options, we were asked if we had anywhere to stay for the night because I strive to live honestly, explained our temporary living arrangement at the hotel. At that point, our hope for guidance and assistance was halted as she explained that she could not offer us help until we no longer had access to the hotel. We would have to come back and start the process again after we checked out. We returned to Brooklyn on what must have the quietest train ride we have ever experienced. What we had just encountered as a couple, and new parents was traumatizing and a lot to process. This experience was more than a reality check; it was a gut punch. When did I become the woman with no resources or backup plan? This event was just the beginning of a process in which God stripped us until all we had was Him. After sharing our jolt to reality at the shelter with a couple of close friends, I was encouraged to find another way to get a roof over our heads because the shelter would be too dangerous. You could imagine with all going on, my husband and I were not on the best of terms at this time, but we were still pressing through for our marriage and family. Everything was happening as we approached our 3rd year of marriage. What an excellent honeymoon phase, right? As we pressed on clinging to the direction of God, we spent a short stay with my in-laws and eventually ended up with an apartment. It happened to be a small one-bedroom apartment that we helped a family member get approved for about four years before needing it ourselves. We thought we were blessing him by finding him a place to stay, but it turned out he was holding our blessing for when we would need it!

From this humble one-bedroom apartment, I held tight to God's promises. He had shown me more than what we had at the time. He showed me being in a position to help others because we possessed more than enough. I just knew with everything in me that this was not the last stop on our journey, so I held on to His promises, and He held me each time I tried to let go. We lived paycheck to paycheck for a few years as I worked tirelessly to build the business God said would flourish. During this time, God gave me a dream that my husband sent me a text letting me know he lost his job. While I was mentally prepared for this to happen, we were far from financially prepared to lose our sole income. A few months after that dream, the dreaded text arrived. He had lost his job and did not know what we were going to do. By the time he came home, I had a whole new business plan ready to go, and it was all I could talk about. I am sure he thought I was having a breakdown at the time but not too long after, my business started turning a profit, and I could take over the bills. To make sure I knew it all came from God, this all happened precisely when my company celebrated its fifth year in business. In retrospect, maybe I should have asked God to make me profitable in 1 year because what I asked, I received.

God likes to show out, and He always does it on time! If I had not stayed the course, if I wallowed in self-pity instead of trusting His process, I would have returned to that shelter and likely threw away my last chance at being a business owner and manifesting His promise over my life. Since we trusted Him without wavering, we now live in a 4-bedroom home in South Carolina. I use my role as a business owner to provide a place for families to generate wealth on their terms and help broaden horizons through exploration of our world. No matter what life is throwing at you or seems to be taking away from you, press into God, hold on and do not let go. He is waiting for you! He did not strip you or correct you because He is displeased with you. You are precious to Him. He does not want to give you the world. He wants to give it back to you!

He is trying to restore you to the glory you were intended to reign in since the beginning of man.

If you don't take anything else from this chapter, remember your weakness is His strength, and the strong hand of the Lord is matchless. Poverty cannot destroy you; addiction cannot have you; restoration is in your weakest moments before God. He heard your cry yesterday, today, and tomorrow! Your tears were your SOS, and God received the message. I agree with you right now that the will of the Father for your life will come to full fruition. There is nothing on this Earth or in the Heavens that can stop you from becoming who God called you to be. Your success is sealed by his hand under the authority of Jesus Messiah; let it be so.

www.nuwavetravel.com

Chapter 6

There is no greater agony than bearing an untold story inside you." Maya Angelou

Silent Truths

By Tanzi Morris

"Have you ever wanted to die?" Manifesting happiness and life into yourself have got to be, by far, one of the hardest things to do. Imagine, for as long as you can remember, bad things just happen to you. Could you imagine the pain, the agony, and tears that come along with being a victim numerous times? I manifested happiness. I decided to no longer believe that I was a victim. I no longer played the role. I no longer expected terrible things to happen. I stopped looking at others for my happiness. Most of all, I stopped blaming God.

I was a victim of child sexual abuse. I always warn others; before understanding who, I am, you must know where I have been. I was young when the abuse began; I say young because I can remember being just 5 years old and being touched. So, although I am unable to recall exactly when the abuse started, I can tell you the abuse continued until I was well into my teens. The sexual abuse is a chapter all in itself, so a trilogy and biography will be released to explain and educate society on my abuse as well as open society's eyes to the untold story of family child sexual abuse.

Some experts say that most victims of child sexual abuse become predators themselves, while others remain victims. Not too long after the sexual abuse, I entered my first real highschool relationship, at only the age of 17. The violent abuse was something I expected, so when it began, I accepted the abuse along with making excuses for the violence. Well into my senior year of high school, my boyfriend I dated for a year began to be violent. He was older, he was popular, but most of all, he was my outlet to get away from my hometown; he was a year older, so after he graduated from our high school, he moved to Atlanta, Georgia, to pursue music and start college. I wanted to erase the sexual abuse I had encountered for so long. Not realizing that it was the abuse that led me to be in such a toxic and abusive relationship and for so long. No matter how bad it was, I hated the sexual abuse memories more. I made plans to move to be with him. I planned my entire life around the abuse and focused on what was more important, starting over.

Life has a funny way of showing you things. Being a victim never looked good on me. Those scars, bruises and tears never looked good, so why accept those things? As a teenager, when I was supposed to be planning for prom dresses, graduation, and college, I was instead covering black eyes, covering bruises from classmates, friends, and my mother. The beatings and bruises became so normal, I began to "disobey" just to get the painful beating, to numb just how hurt and unhappy I was with life. I remember on several occasions, hoping he would beat me to death. This way, those horrible memories of who I was could go away. You see, by this age, although I was hurting from my secret, I also began to blame myself. Not sure of how it was my fault, I blamed my entire existence. Because if I had not been born, none of these things would have happened, right? Funny thing is that I genuinely believed that well into my 20s. This abuse only came to a violent and sudden end two years later because my boyfriend lost his temper publically and gave me an asswhooping that knocked me to my senses. Now think of the most open and public place to lose your temper; you guessed it, Wal-Mart. A secret that I had kept for so long had finally been exposed! I wanted to DIE! Classmates, coworkers, even strangers now knew my secret! So, what did I do? I played the victim. My entire world had changed overnight! Well, the boyfriend was caught, given probation and we never spoke again.

Although this relationship was over, I needed someone to love me. I found love in a friendship that bloomed into 16 years and two children later. But man, the pain and patience it took us over the years. You see, the sexual and violent abuse ended, but all the pain and baggage that I was not healed from was brought into my new relationship. Our very first argument, I remember flinching when he put his hands in the air. He stopped the argument and assured me that he was not going to hit me. You see, people do not understand that when someone goes through a trauma, that person must heal. Finding that hurt, confronting the hurt are all steps to healing. Mine just so happen to take therapy and lots of praying. Over the next few years in my 20s, I began to realize the root of my pain. I began to openly express my pain, my past, and this allowed me to not only address my trauma but confront it also. This openness, felt like a weight had been lifted off my shoulders. I was able to stand a bit taller, walk with a little bit more confidence.

Being a young Black woman struggling with identity issues is tough. I went through physical and mental insecurities because I was not taught or shown self-love. Learning how to love myself was the first step. Self-evaluating what was wrong and dealing with those issues. Some women will say it is already inside of us; others may say that it is something we are taught. Whichever way is right, I did not have either advantage. I was a broken little girl still trying to figure out life as well try to move on from my past trauma. Most of my adult friendships and relationships suffered because of my disadvantages. My husband and I have mountains of highs and lows in our marriage because we both dealt with our own issues and it affected our marriage tremendously. Every issue was individually addressed and released. I like to use an onion as an example because I had so many layers of pain to sort and address. Seeing the growth, the pain be released and let go. It felt amazing!

I will admit there were struggles. Being human, we are bound to make mistakes. There were times I would get discouraged and even feel defeated with my past because the trauma goes that deep. That is when I seeked any alternative that could assist with healing. I spoke to therapists, coaches, wrote in my journal and probably sang every woman empowering R&B

song ever written to try to sort through the pain I still felt after all these years. Deciding not to open up to friends or relatives about what I was dealing with was a choice because I was the strong one. I was the one everyone came to when there was a problem. I was the one that was supposed to have it all together. At least, that is what I told myself. Being the oldest of five, you kind of automatically take on this role as the responsible one to make sure everyone is ok and everything gets done. That is my life. This has been my role my entire life, so this is obviously what I was put here for, right? Struggling with those thoughts, the healing process took me longer than it may take others.

Now you will notice I have not mentioned God. Some will want to know why. You see, as a child and well into my 20s, I struggled with faith. Because if there was a God, there is no way He would have let my childhood be taken away from me. If there was a God, there is no way I would have endured such violence and there is absolutely no way my siblings would have been placed into foster care. God and I have been through a lot also. And when you hear that old saying, "Well, God knows my heart." The truth is, He really does! It took several near-death experiences, a few more heartaches and tears that began my questioning and talking to God. As an adult, the love-hate relationship that I had established with God began to evolve. He would let me know that I needed Him, and He was watching over me. Over time, I survived a house fire, my siblings being placed into foster care, gaining custody of those siblings, surviving a car fire, and going against all the odds, becoming a wife and mother, which I was told I would never become. All those pains and gains brought me closer to God. I began to talk to Him. I stopped questioning Him and began asking Him. Some days are better than others, and even now, well into my 30s, me and God, we talk daily. Once I forgave myself, I was able to let go and let God!

I enjoy speaking openly about my story to young women because I went against all odds. I am not my past. I am not my environment, and we truly can do anything we put our minds to. I am an advocate for domestic abuse survivors because they do not have a voice until something happens. I want women to know they are not alone. Any person that is in an abusive relationship should know that you can make it without them. I became a Massage Therapist to remind victims of abuse that physical touch is ok and safe. I want people with young children in their families to listen to your children. If they give signs that they are uncomfortable, listen to those signs. The worst thing you can do to a child is not protect them. Finding out of their abuse and hiding it or "sweeping it under the rug," will destroy that child!

My name is Tanzi Morris. I am a survivor. I am a writer, Author, Entrepreneur, Business Owner, Wife and Mother. In 2020, Covid-19 hit our nation hard. Along with this pandemic, I became pregnant; so, the world became different. I no longer was able to provide massages, provide love through touch.

Back to the drawing board, right? July 2021, I will be launching my very own, Hair/Beauty and barber supply delivery service. Being my own boss and being there for my children has always been my goal. Along with my delivery service, there will be a hair/wig and lash collection, along with beauty products, to be available for US shipping. The goal is to provide beauty to anyone in a dash, and I am claiming to God and the atmosphere to eventually open my very own physical beauty store.

You see, once I began to tell my story, forgiving myself and speaking to God, that was when my life changed. I claimed that I was going to be happy no matter what. I spoke happiness. I accepted happiness and for the first time, I was expecting happiness. My life changed. My marriage changed. I no longer was a victim. Once I let go of that role, life as I once knew it was changed. It does not matter the journey; all that matters is your destination and the impact you make along the way.

www.serenebeautymore.com

Chapter 7

Coach Tina Ramsay

The Tina Ramsay Show

(Epic Business Leaders)

"Now to each one the manifestation of the Spirit is given for the common good".

1 Corinthians 12:7

Know your Worth and Manifesting the Queen that you are!

Every great moment, every breakthrough, and every thought that will become the start of something EPIC starts with you. Before you can tap into this and operate within your God-Given Greatness, you have to first believe and understand who you are. You are Royalty! You are Born a Queen!

Do you truly understand who You Are? Let me feel you in on something; you don't need to have a King in order to be a Queen. A Queen isn't defined by money, a fictional character read in a book or seen in a movie. A True Queen is any Woman regardless of her background, color, or education. A

Queen is not controlled but she allows her past to create her why and tell her story of how she was able to overcome, make moves, and help others. A Queen is You and your Ability to see and believe yourself as such. A mindset of self-love, growth, and self-worth. When someone called me a Queen in the past, I felted uncomfortable because I felt unworthy of that title. Now, I know that I not only deserve this title, but I also embody this title because I was born a Queen and so are you! I now know my worth and I am embracing it. ALL WOMEN ARE QUEENS, not just me. So, in order for you to take and manifest your true purpose in life, you first have to know your value. No One Can Do This for You. This is a journey that you can only take with yourself and God. This starts with you developing the proper mindset about yourself. YOU ARE A QUEEN!

Manifest what you WANT

On December 20, 2020, my business direction changed forever with just five words. (Tina, you need to Focus) these were the words that a popular Informical Queen that sold 2.5 billion dollars of products spoke directly to me. As an entrepreneur, we are usually running more than one business at a time. I was running three businesses that all included multiple layers that needed my constant attention. But one of these businesses was the foundation of starting all of my successes and it was hard to let go. I knew what needed to be done but I was afraid to do it. So, my question was, how can I put that business on hold to focus on just one thing. I have Never Done just One thing in all of my Life. So how can I take Forbes's advice and just do one thing? Especially when that one thing is so different.

You See, my other businesses kept me drained, stressed, overmanaged, felt under-appreciated, overworked, and underpaid. My Effort, Hardwork, and Time were not even covering my family's monthly expenses at this point and was helping so many other people. At this point, I could not even help myself. I asked myself what I was doing because this path was so clear to me before but now, I am confused. What once brought me joy and driven my passion in my businesses was now bringing me sadness that had me in a business depression. I was left feeling confused, distracted all the time, questioning why I am here and should I continue. The purpose that was once so clear to me was not the same. I thought that I had this part figured out but yet again, I reach another crossroad.

I was in one of my many personal development classes and the speaker said that you have to ASK the Universe for what You Want. I was Universe well … I will ask GOD who is my everything and tell Him what I want. She said that you can not just say a blanket statement. You have to be clear, detailed, and precise on what it is that you WANT. Now, this was not easy for me because I felt like I was doing something wrong.

But I decided to give it a try because I was sick and tired of the situation at the time.

So, I started being precise, clear, and direct to exactly what I wanted in detail. I spoke it, I wrote down, I read it, I pray for it, I sang it, and I Manifested it! Yes, I can officially say that you hold the key within yourself to manifest whatever you desire and want in your life. Believe it and operate within it. You will see that it will happen. The first time it happened to me, I was like WOW!

When Your Manifestation Path Changes

In the pit of my stomach, I knew that my Mission was shifting in a new direction of manifestation that I wasn't familiar with in order to help my family and others. I knew that this new path would make a positive impact in the world on a global scale. I prayed about it and my answer scared me. Because I knew that I had to Focus on this new completely different business. I was afraid to walk away or put on hold the comfort I felt of knowing my other businesses inside and out. Walking through this unknown door that only allowed two people to go through Myself and God Only! This was a Mission that started with me saying what I wanted through prayer. When I received my answer, I didn't like the answer, so I prayed again, again, and again the same answer; the assignment increased but the start remained the same. I knew that I had to act. It wasn't about me anymore, but I was being used as a vessel for the greater good.

To start this New Mission myself and God were the only two people allowed to go through this door of opportunity. I had to surrender to the process and allow God to direct and align me with the right people to carry out this Assigned Mission He has given me to help Entrepreneurs. This would take Sacrifice, Manifesting, Focus, Trust, Learning, and Faith to start, continue, and complete this assignment that will change the history of entrepreneurs worldwide faster, making a virtual impact. Starting with just this one seed that will yield a massive harvest over time to last throughout multiple generations.

This is not just a Mission but a Movement of History Changing Purpose. A movement for Who? Entrepreneurs. For whom? Women and Men. Why is this so significant and took a lot to do for me? It is because my main businesses were All Female Based Only, No Men. I had to wrestle with my emotions in regard to changing my complete brand and worried about my female audience feeling abandon. But, something started to change; more men were attracted to the uplifting, educational, positive teaching and coaching that I provided. I started to notice that men were sharing my wellness and business tips. I noticed that more men signed up to be coached by me on business and social media. They were engaging and sharing my post on social media. They were watching my live videos on social media, purchasing my classes, recommended it, tuning in to my TV show and podcast. Then Men started reaching out for Business Strategist Coaching, Facebook Training, MLM Direct Sale Training, Branding Help, and supporting me in helping ones in need within the community. Then one day, my husband pulled me aside and said help the men too, out of the blue. I was praying about it but never said anything to my husband about it. Then two of my male friends said Tina, I love what you are doing for women, but men need you in our corner to build us up and teach us too. That gave me all the confirmation that I need to move forward in algin with my purpose that was manifesting itself right before my eyes.

Building a Platform for an Epic EBL Movement

The change took months to implement, transition, branding, and social media development. In season 2, we revealed the new name of our TV Show. We explained that we would no longer be called Heal the Honeypot TV that's only for Women but we will now be called The Tina Ramsay Show and Podcast is now a platform to motivate Men and Women. Although our name changed, our Purpose and Mission has not changed. We are just focusing on helping Entrepreneurs Excel in Business, Wellness, and Life. The Tina Ramsay Show and

Podcast is all about Spotlighting standout amazing men and women entrepreneurs that are coming together sharing upbuilding knowledge centered around business, wellness, and life that is making a positive impact in the world.

Later, we revealed what I prayed, the answer, and what manifested from what I wanted that in essence, created a movement to provide entrepreneurs with what they want.

Becoming what you Want and Manifest.

Walking into my personal Manifestation second door took me to a place where God allowed me to bring other people with me and I thank him for this. I love to be of service to others. My personal want manifested itself for me to be positioned by God to become the Founder and CEO of EBL Epic Business Leaders, which is an upbuilding supportive community for Entrepreneurs to receive the support, opportunities, connections, networking, collaborations, resources, services, lead generation, and visibility they want/need to excel and grow their businesses. I know personally that it does not matter how great your product or services are if we don't know that you exist. Our Epic Business Leaders Team makes it affordable for you to be seen and known on social media and beyond. We build your influence & credibility, making you the go-to within your niche market. Our Epic Business Leaders Community is Sponsored by The Tina Ramsay. We literally have access with God's help 40+ TV Shows, Podcasts, Magazines, Book Publishing houses, Sony, Social Media Management, Lawyers, Graphics and Merch designers, TV Production, PR, Speaking Engagements, and so much more. We are blessed to be affiliated, collaborating, and networking with some of the biggest people within multiple industries of business from Entrepreneurship, Major Influencers, Public speakers, Coaches, and Entertainment within our network of influence. We are grateful and thankful to God for positioning us so that we can help to position and elevate you.

The Blessing of Surrendering to the Process and Manifesting what you wanted!

Now, I understand that all of my previous failures and successes in businesses were just a steppingstone, not a permanent place, that led me to the EBL Epic Business Leaders Movement & The Tina Ramsay Show. The confusion, the roller coaster of feeling, the trials, and dropping to my lowest moment in life & business. All of this makes sense now. The quote from Napoleon Hill is becoming clearer every moment where he says," 'Every adversity, every failure, every heartache carries with it the seed of an equal or greater benefit.' Understand that in order for you to manifest your present and future, you have to leave that past behind. When you are constantly hitting adversity, challenges, and struggles that make you want to give up. DO NOT DO THAT! Just be more direct on what it is that you want to manifest and walk in it. You are on the verge of your biggest breakthrough yet!

I had to get out of my own way and take myself out of the driver's seat of my life and allow God to do the driving. Once I did that, God then aligned me with the right people to work out what I wanted and to complete the assignment that He gave me to do. You will have people come into your life to teach you a lesson, take you one step farther, distract you, or completely take you to the table you need to be at in order for you to make the moves that you are purposed to do within the area of what you believe and manifest for yourself. I am only the messenger; the vessel being used to leverage the playing field for small business entrepreneurs to get cost-effective quality marketing opportunities and resources to truly Level Them UP when they join our Epic Business Leaders Community doing it the eZWay.

I am now known and recognized in Celebrity A-List communities for my work on TV, Hosting, and Podcasting. Did I do all of this? No! God did this for me and I thank Him every day. Manifesting and Surrendering to His process allowed Him to use me for His purpose, mission, and movement to help Entrepreneurs Worldwide using my influence and connections through Him to open the door for

You like so many have done for me. Are you ready to take your seat?

My Tip:

Manifest, Focus & Surrender to God's Purpose for you!

Help others and watch your Blessings Overflow!

Use the Gifts that He gave you to Impact the World for Good

&

Bless Yourself & Family Financially.

Manifesting Excellence Bio:

Coach Tina is an Awarded Honoree Certified Coach, Businesswoman, and Sort After International Public Speaker that has been featured on ABC, NBC, CBS, Fox, Magazines, books. TV, and radio. She's a proud mother of two children, a wife of almost 20 years, and relies on her Strong Faith & Relationship with God to Direct her steps. She's an Accomplished Editorial Columnist writer for 4 Magazines, Associate TV Producer & Podcast Specialist for eZWay Network, Executive Producer & Host of The Tina Ramsay Show and Podcast, which is an IMDb accredited TV Show, 2X Best-Selling Contributing Author on Amazon, and the CEO of Epic Business Leaders which is a Business and

Community to position Entrepreneurs with support, coaching, resources, connections, collaborations, and quality cost-effective services for small businesses to maximize their visibility to generate leads through the EBL network, partnerships, and collaborations with leaders within the industry. She's also the CEO of HealTheHoneypot.com, a Female Natural Wellness Online Business. Coach Tina and her team Want Spotlight Entrepreneurs to Come Share, Shine, and Grow on her show and their EBL Community. We help you understand your worth and how to start operating in your God-given gifts to bless others and themselves by positively impacting the world with good through group and private coaching. We dare you to Manifest, Focus, and Monetize your God-Given Gifts, Unapologetically not undermining your worth so that you and others will win!

Website: TheTinaRamsayShow.com

Email: TheTinaRamsayShow1@gmail.com

Social Media: Youtube, Facebook & Instagram: The Tina Ramsay Show

Photo Credit: Multifarious Studio

Join FREE Epic Business Leaders Facebook Group Today and Do it the eZWay!

Chapter 8

Chapter name: Mirror Mirror on the wall; who do you say I am?

By Dianna Scott

Have you ever struggled with self-image and or self-esteem? Although the enemy will make you feel like you are alone because you have felt this way. Know that you are not alone. Let me explain my journey on seeing myself through God's eyes. 85% of the world's population is affected by low self-esteem, according to Dr. Joe Rubino.

I decree and declare that you will see yourself through God's eyes by the end of this chapter.

Today people would describe me as bold, confident, and empowering. Today, I love myself and I see myself the way that God sees me. I am who God says I am. I can do what He says I can do. But that wasn't always the case.

In high school, I hated mirrors. I avoided them at all costs. I mean, why would anyone want to look in the mirror if they looked like me? My face was too fat, and my nose was way too big. When I went into public restrooms, I would look down as I washed my hands. And if someone came beside me and started washing their hands, I would look in the mirror and pretend to fix my hair so that I didn't have to look myself in the mirror.

I remember wrapping a rubber band around my nose and going to sleep in hopes of waking up with a smaller nose. I would cry and cry to God, saying "Why didn't you make me pretty?" I would close my eyes and imagine I was someone else.

I got to a place that I was so emotionally low. I started to think of thoughts like, "why am I even here." I realized I was getting to a place of no return. God began to draw me. I started to cry out to God; as I was basking in His presence, the holy brought back to my remembrance of who He said I was.

Fast forward to college. I was determined that I was going to accept me and love me for me. Slowly but surely, I started to fall back into not liking what I see in the mirror and not only that. I begin to compare myself to everyone around me. I started telling myself I wasn't pretty enough, I wasn't smart enough, I just wasn't enough.

Here I was repeating the cycle again. I wondered if it would always be like this. I came across and quote that said." She remembered who she was, and the game changed as I was thinking about that over and over.

God told me to look in the mirror and tell myself who He says that I am and to repeat it. So, I began to do this Day after day and month after month, I was feeling like this was pointless and I was wasting my time. I started to tell myself this is not working. And why even do this. I still don't like the way I look. My nose is still too big.

I started to read Bible verses on who God says I am.

A few months later, I was praying and worshipping, and God began to speak to me. He said,

You are my daughter.

You are loved.

you were created in my image, so that makes you marvelous.

You are my workmanship.

in other words, you are a work of art.

https://www.facebook.com/dianna.scott.39

Chapter 9

Conscientious Lies

By Faith Ricardson

It all started when I was in kindergarten. It was around October 1989, and I would always tell my parents that I wanted my room like a doctor's office, and by the time I would come home from school, they made it happen for me. As I got older and entered high school, I always reminded myself to just be myself. By the time I was 16, I got pregnant with my son as a junior in high school. I was in an abusive relationship, and I finally told my parents while they were in church. I had no choice. I was 17, scared, pregnant, and I was tired of being beaten every day for absolutely nothing. Going forward, I finally got my own place when I was 19. I got pregnant again in 2002 when my son was about 9 months old. That pregnancy was high risk. I bled every single day, I was at the doctor at least 3 times a week, and at first, they couldn't find the amniotic sac until I was 12 weeks pregnant. I went into imminent delivery when I was 28 weeks pregnant, on February 18th, 2003. I had my daughter in the car on the way to the hospital. When I got there, the responders and nurses acted like they were scared to take me out of the car, so my boyfriend had to do that and put me on the gurney. As he was checking me in at the front desk, one of the doctors come in and takes my daughter out of my pants, puts her in a pink basin, and tells me that she has passed away. My daughter, Ja'Niyah Shan'Tayiah Lee, died on February 18th, 2003, at 5:54p.m., the day before my birthday. I have not celebrated my birthday since 2003 because I have that vision in my head still of my daughter in that pink basin in the middle of my bed. I was no good after that. I was depressed and in pain all the time. I finally made an appointment to see a doctor, and of course, they ran every test on me known to man to see what the issue was. Well… come to find out, I was diagnosed with fibromyalgia and thyroid disease at 19. My body was hurting so bad; the inflammation, the flare-ups, and me constantly losing weight was something that I couldn't get used to. I had dropped down to 93 pounds, and some people thought I was on drugs, which wasn't the case. I honestly think that, along with having fibromyalgia, being beaten all the time, from having 2 broken wrists, 3 fractured ribs, black eyes, the right side of my face broken, being stomped on, pushed into bushes, being spit at in the face, having liquor thrown in my face, being picked up and slammed all the time, had a tremendous effect on my body.

In July 2006, I got pregnant again, but this time, it was a tubal pregnancy. That was the most painful thing that I had ever been through. That same month, my heart was broken into a million pieces. I had never been so depressed, sad, and miserable in my entire life. I didn't even go outside for about 1 year. All I did was cry, drink coffee, and smoke cigarettes. I made the choice to see my psychiatrist, and he put me on

Xanax, Zoloft, and Klonopin. When I took these prescribed medications, it felt like what I was going through at that time had surpassed me, and I didn't feel depressed, sad; I didn't want to cut myself anymore, and I felt free from the pain and hurt that I was going through. In turn, I knew the side effects of this medication. It was doing more harm than good to me, so after 3 years of being dependent on them, I decided it was time to stop. I came to my senses after I passed out at Walgreens in front of my children, and the EMT's had to do chest compressions on me to bring me back. After that incident, I stopped cold turkey. It was one of the worst experiences that I have ever felt in my entire life. I couldn't eat, couldn't sleep, I had tremors and felt very uneasy. Those were the withdrawal symptoms of benzodiazepines. I knew what I was doing when I completely stopped instead of being weaned off them. I was so pale and very frail at that time because I depended on them to mask the pain that I was feeling for all those years. I was raised as a church girl, so I turned to my Bible and to God. He was my strength besides my children and my parents.

While I was in college full-time, taking a course overload that consisted of 11 classes, I was taking care of my father, who had dementia, with two children while working a part-time job. I just kept pushing and going even harder so that my family could see me graduate. I was the first child of both my parents to graduate college. My father didn't have a chance to even finish the 3rd grade. He was born and raised in Painter, Virginia. He told me the story so many times about how the farm owner told him while he was walking to school that his farm needed to be tended to, or my father, his mother, and his sisters wouldn't have anywhere to live. That's when the unthinkable happened. He slapped the schoolbooks out of my father's hand. This was back in 1937 when my father was just 9 years old. My father was beyond happy when he saw me walk across that stage in 2013. He passed away on March 2, 2015. That really broke my heart. My father was my best friend. We did almost everything together. But I had to be strong for my mother and my children. They are all I have left that I can say that truly and genuinely cares about me. My children and I are very close. And I thank God for them every single moment and day of my life.

    I honestly thank God for bringing me through the tough times in my life. I never for once thought that people could be so indignant, so narcissistic, and so spiteful to someone who has never disrespected them or done no harm in any way possible. That depression and all of that crying that I did years ago over people and what they did to me turned into hate and anger. I have never had so much hate and anger within my heart, soul and mind. I remember staying up for long periods of time just thinking to myself, talking to myself, just beyond mad to the point that I had a stroke over people and their malicious ways. This happened on my daughter's 11th birthday last year. I still have nerve damage from that stroke. And I let myself get that angry to the point that I had a stroke because of what some people had done to me. From that point on, I had to change the way I thought, processed, and reacted to situations. I know that it is a sin to hate, and I am telling you that it took everything in me and beyond me to try and let it go. At the end of the day, I have let it go because I need to move on with my life, but I promise you this…... I will never, ever forget what was done to me. I suffer from excessive hypertension, and I take 4 blood pressure pills a day to ensure that it goes down, but that's not the case. Now I'm taking a total of 14 pills a day for high cholesterol, hyperthyroidism, hypertension, depression, bipolar disorder, fibromyalgia, and heart medication. From all the extensive training that I've had, all the certifications, degrees, late nights studying and drinking coffee… My goal is to help someone change their habits, new or old, and allow them to see their selves from a new perspective in life. I am 2 years away from becoming a Doctor of Natural and Integrative Medicine. This thing called life is beyond beautiful and amazing. I haven't traveled the world yet, but if you can open your eyes wide enough, there is so much beauty around us!! From the grass to the trees, to the rivers and ponds, to the birds and the bees, to the flowers and plants, to the people, places and things. I see the beauty in everything. It brings about a new vision and view on life and just how precious it really is. I love and react to every single moment in my life because the next day isn't promised to anyone. I took an oath when I became a member and Soror of Alpha Omega Theta Sorority, Incorporated, and that is to serve mankind. I want and need people to feel and know that they are loved, valued, and respected... regardless of color, ethnicity, gender, sexuality or affiliations. We are all interconnected because we are one…. The Human Race.

www.essenceofintegrativehealth.com

Chapter 10

Manifesting Excellent

By Katina Davis

This was an experience that turned into a mighty testimony in my Life! Here's my side of the truth.

My prayer would Be Lord, please send my husband where is he? My mornings M-F I was Up early and ready to go. I attended college for medical billing/coding. I finally felt like I was accomplishing my goals which keep me pushing, focused. I loved learning and meeting others from all over the world who also has ambitions, and positive energy. I worked in the college financial aid office as a file clerk. The only thing missing was my King.

I always dreamed of that fairy tale wedding with my King standing at the altar awaiting his Queen. But I would soon find out that every fairy tale doesn't have a happy ending! My birthday was coming up and I was overjoyed about celebrating my big 31" so my cousin and sister-in-law decided to take me out. We went to a nightclub we laughed, danced the night turned out better than I expected. While we were dancing, I noticed this sexy tatted-up young man playing pool. My eyes couldn't stay off of him, hoping he didn't notice me, but he did, our eyes locked in and it went from there. When he approached me, he said his name, we talked for a while. He told me about himself and his daughter but when he said I'm looking for a wife, I'm ready to be a family man, my heart melted. At the end of the night, we exchanged numbers. I was caught off guard with his reply because I was also looking for my soul mate. Days had gone by with no calls from my new friend, so I decided to call him; when he answered, I said I just wanted to make sure you're okay, he replied to me, thanks, never had anyone to call and just check on me. He was out of town working, we talked everyday on phone like we were high school sweetheart. We talked for hours and hours at a time. He told me stories of his childhood of not feeling loved by his parents. My childhood was similar been raised in foster care then by my grandparents. We both just wanted to be loved. After weeks of talking over the phone, he asked me to marry him, and I said Yes! We decided to get married when he returned from working on May 27. On the morning of his return, so much was going wrong, just one thing after another. There was an auto accident which caused a delay in his arrival time. When he arrived, it was 10 mins till our wedding, and he still had to get dressed. Then we heard the worst news a soon-to-be bride could have heard. We were told, you have to reschedule because we were 7 mins late. I broke down crying. I couldn't understand how this was happening. All kind of thoughts were going through my mind. What was God trying to show me? At that moment, I really know something wasn't right, so I started paying closer attention to our relationship/him. In the beginning, everything was good we both loved to talk on the phone we enjoyed each other's company. I started praying, asking God to show me if he was for me. We did our family events, movie night. What I do know is you better be ready when you ask God to show you cause he will reveal it to you. I didn't know why he would excuse me of things when he was out of town working. He would call all day while he was at work, saying I have men there or men calling me. The only way he felt like nothing was going on was to stay on the phone. He would tell his family that I was cheating on him. My excuse I keep telling myself he just needs me to show him love, so I stayed, thinking he would eventually change. Hiding behind my pain/tears in front of my children but really, they know mama wasn't happy. They would always come up, hug me and say, I love you. But One thing I do know is when they start saying you're cheating, you better keep both eyes open and don't blink. There was a lot of verbal abuse, I couldn't leave the house without him wanting to go; it was cool sometimes, but A Queen needed to breathe cause he was like the energizer bunny. He would keep going and going all night, auguring till it became draining. When I go back thinking about our 1st child together, he was so ecstatic when he found out I was pregnant with our 1st child, a baby princess! He did everything a woman would want during her pregnancy, back rubs, late-night store runs, he even cried when I gave birth to her! She was he's little princess, he couldn't put her down. Shortly after her birth, I started noticing things again, which made me question him but he would also try to flip it and excuse me of things been up my past, just straight try and make me think I was Crazy. I knew God was showing me these things for a reason. I prayed and asked, and it was hurtful thinking the one who's supposed to love and protect was secretly trying to destroy me. I watched his words and actions, the things he wished on me would happen to him. The mental abuse was worse than the physical abuse. Imagine not knowing what kind of day each day would be having to be on edge about saying the wrong thing simply and he would blow it into something dramatic. I was overwhelmed and I started to break me down. I was in a depression and didn't know. I couldn't sleep, eat, stayed in bed nauseous all day. My weight drop, my hair started falling out, teeth started to crack. I was changing before my eyes. I didn't wanna go out around people/family. He would tell me no man will marry you with 7 children. You have stretch marks, you're not going to be shit. He tried everything to break me. All my dreams and ideas didn't even matter to him, it was all about his dreams. So I set aside my dreams to help him bring his dreams to reality. Nothing I did was ever good enough for him. I was asking God why Me. I love this man, I'm faithful and loyal to him. Why? I was Tied and Tied of not feeling appreciated by someone I'm giving my all to. I had no friends or family to talk with. He got caught up and went to prison for 2 years. I waited on him and was celibate, working, holding it down until he got out. I visited him every weekend, phone calls everyday, and money on his books. He gets out and shows no loyalty back to me or his kids. He was secretly planning to leave us. Things were not good when he got out. I didn't know if he needed to readjust to society or what. My mind was in disbelief at his actions. How can someone do that to the only one who's been there. An argument broke out with him telling me that my parents wasn't shit so I wasn't going to be shit, he said that I would be dead before him because I was the one with diabetes. But you love your family. My mind started racing, does this man really love me? Is this love? My father (God) would soon put all the pieces together on Why Me. I'm home in bed, not feeling well when I received a phone call from his sister telling me he had gotten shot and was paralyzed from his waist down. I couldn't take in what I was hearing, my heart dropped. I prayed on my way to the hospital that this wasn't real. He was in ICU recovering from open-heart surgery. Seeing him like that crushed my heart. I had to pick up his property from the police station. This is where the pieces started to fit the missing spaces. Dude was about to start a whole new life with another woman and her children. I found text, message, voice message, videos. I was devastated, I felt stupid, used, betrayed. I felt like he was going to leave me and his kids for dead. I was pregnant with our third child together. I miscarried from all the stress I was going through. Traveling back and forward to the hospital out of town while he was there for 6 months. Having to explain to my children what had happened to their dad was something I've never thought I would do. I had to put away the hurt on top of the pain of find out all the pillow talks /talks about his homeboys' cheating on their babyma's and the different women they were sleeping with was his stories/lies that he told me. The hardest Pain to endure is the betrayal of LOVE. Even after finding out his little secrets, I still drove to see him, not cause of love for him anymore but because of My heart, God made me this way. I was on assignment for God, I didn't even know but because of my heart. I was obedient to my Father's (God) voice. I visited him in hospital. His mom helped her out with him, take the kids to see him, nursing home. His mind frame, actions didn't change at all with him now being parlayed. God allowed these things to happen, not for me to feel pain but to know when it's real or fake. God showed me who's for me and who's against me. He removed put replaced. I've had favor through this. The enemy wanted me to turn my heart & be bitter and angry.

I didn't understand why God chose me to go through these things. As time went on, God showed me All the supernatural events He was doing in my Favor behind the scenes to bring me out of that horrible situation. No, I couldn't understand. I was trying to put things together on my own, but I should've been leaning not on my own understanding but Gods! When tragic situations happen in our lives, it doesn't always mean it's bad most of the time, it's because God has A Bigger and Better plan/blessing for our life. You just have to trust Him through your process. Believe me, God makes no mistakes!!! He's an on-time God. My father (God) didn't allow me to fall but to come out of the fire a Queen.

https://www.facebook.com/katina.davis.397

Chapter 11

God gave us a way out of

The Dark-Manifest the Light of Jesus Christ

John 8:12

"I am the light of the world."

By Mary Angel

Throughout of our life, we all had Darkness trying to take over us our

entire life, especially our minds. Satan, because of sin and fallen men and women, we are in a world system that's very wicked and very dark. The reason behind the darkness is sin that we as humanity are subjected to if we are not accepting the redemption of the way our precious heavenly loving God is everything we need to be. Children of the light also able to manifest Jesus Christ's excellence through the power of the holy ghost, who is our comforter, teacher, and our guide to all truth, which is the light of Christ Jesus that automatically removes all darkness and dark spirits, dark children of Satan of all witchcraft voodoo hoodoo santira eat. Negative words people who are agents of Satan in your family, on your job, in the grocery store, schools, doctor's office, and even sitting in the church's house looking to stop you from manifesting the light of Jesus Christ. That at any time you walk in repentance and the love and truth of God. The Father of Abraham, Isaac, and Jacob later named in Israel Jehova Jireh, will provide the most important things in our lives that we truly need. And that the light of the love of God our heavenly Father and freedom from darkness of the mind from the negative messages from unseen demons trying to control your entire life. If your mind is black full of no manifestation of Jesus Christ light, Satan's agents can make your darkness feel like you're physically blind and can not see, therefore cursing more darkness to come shut the light out in your entire life. On your light to see where you're going and what you're doing and should be doing. You must call His name, think His light automatically comes and rescues you. If you are walking in the manifestation of the immediate light that's ready to shine so bright and expel the darkness, you have to completely focus and embrace the light and watch Jesus Christ begin to manifest excellence in every area of your life if you give Him the switch that we shouldn't touch because we cut off the light when we start to manifest. Without Jesus Christ to manifest excellence, you must stay away from the switch and Jesus will light Your life with His Excellence. I made it out of the darkness of foster care, divorce, and covid-19. Jesus is the light of the world and remember always that there is no Darkness, nothing that can't be removed from the darkness. He will keep your candle lit.

Let's Manifest Excellence

www.maryangel.org

Chapter 12

What Is Manifesting to Me?

By Myechia Barnett

I have manifested a lot of things, but I did not do it alone. I really had to my faith to work while placing actions behind it. It started with a thought. The first step was believing that I deserved it. The second step was writing it down and presenting what I wanted to God. The third step was meditating on the thoughts of these things. Even when things did not look like I want, I still take a moment and visualize that I already have what I asked for. See, God automatically Provides for us the things we need because that is His promise to us as His children. He also promised to give us the desires of our hearts. In this, you must do some work because He wants to meet you halfway. The fourth step was believing that God could do it. I have been in so many hardships, and it took my belief in Him, that He could do these things even though my situation did not look like it at all. See sometimes; God wants to see what we are willing to do to make the necessary changes needed to make the things we want to happen. Are you willing to take those steps for the changes you want?

When I write on a notepad, notebook, and pen, I start with, "I am so happy and grateful for ……." In Jesus name, Amen. I present what I am grateful for in a way to show God that although I don't currently have it, I believe and see it as if I do. Faith, right? Most importantly, I write what I am grateful for in reference to what I currently have. See, you must have a spirit of gratitude where you are as well as being grateful for the things you do not but want. Do not allow what you are currently going through to stop you from creating your life of prosperity and abundance. It starts with your mind, then believing, and lastly, putting it into action. For example: Let us say you need a place of your own. Start with thinking about what you want. Do you want a 1 bedroom or 2 bedrooms? Do you want a house or apartment? Do you want an area that is quiet and peaceful? Do you want it to be clean? Do you want your rent to be a certain amount? Do you want God to show up supernaturally even if it looks like you cannot afford it right now? Write it down. "I am so happy and grateful for my new 2-bedroom apartment that brings me peace. In Jesus name, Amen." Put a date on it! When do you see this happening beyond what you think or see? Start looking at places. Rent.com or apartments.com (putting in work) Start applying for applications and allow God to lead you. See it. Are you working? What income do you have? Start applying for jobs that will start you off in the bracket that you can pay your rent. Continue to think about what you want. Ask God to show you what to do and where to go, but you must be ready to LISTEN! Obedience will take you farther than you think. Trust me, I know. See that thing through. Below are some examples of what I manifested that I could share. These methods work. My question to you is, what are YOU willing to try God for?

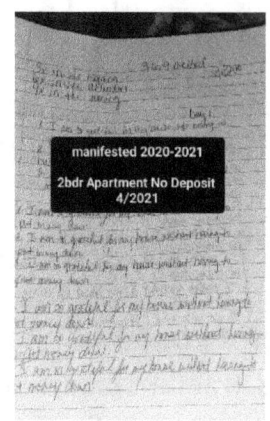

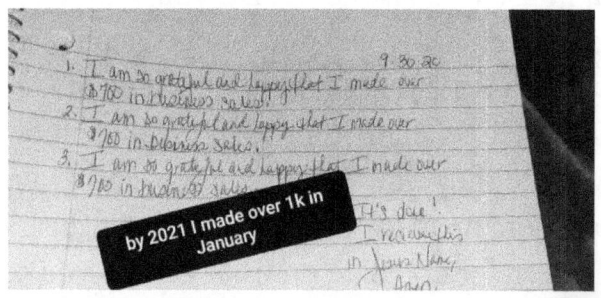

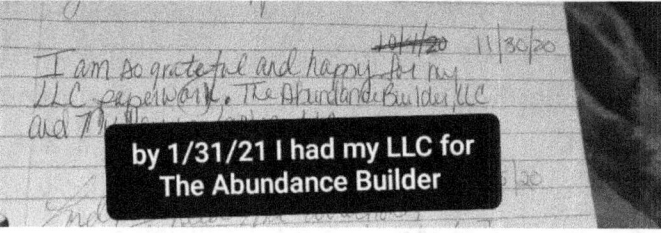

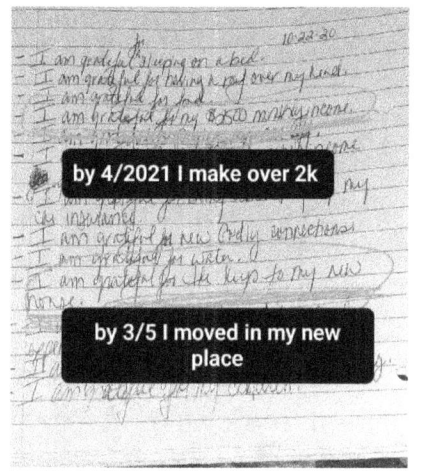

Myechia Barnett

www.myechiabarnett.com

www.theabundancebuilder.com

Thank you so much for reading our book. We all hope this was helpful to you wherever you are on your journey to excellence. Please submit reviews on Amazon and tell the world how this book helped you. Below are some helpful scriptures on manifesting and faith. God bless you and your family and may God bring Prosperity and Abundance to you in all areas of your life. Reach out to the authors of this book and follow them. They are awesome women, and I am grateful to be connected to such amazing queens.

__Honorees__

Why are they being honored? These amazing women were chosen for a special reason. We have many people in our life that played a part in our success or how we got to where we are, even if it is bad. The women on this list played a positive role in my life, from the smallest gestures and some big. Read about them, follow them, and contact them.

The first woman I must honor on this planet is my mother. We all have stories, but we only get one mom. Joanne Davis gave birth to me on Dec. 7, 1989, and everything has a purpose from the moment we are born. If she did not give birth to me, this book would not have happened. I am so grateful she chose to do it. I am grateful she is still here and that I have a chance to put a smile on her face whenever I can. Honor your mother while she is here, no matter what. You will never get another chance once she is called home.

Aiechia Davis, The Water Girl.

Aiechia is my cousin on both sides lol, first cousin on both sides at that. Her mother is my dad's sister, and her father is my mom's brother. I was named after her by her mother, my auntie. I am honoring her because she came back into my life almost 2 years ago and since then, she has blessed me tremendously when no one else could not or would not. We have been inseparable since. I am honoring her for her kind words of inspiration and the role she played in my life, I have watched her grow in hers. She is now an amazing entrepreneur and has taken off in her business. She is profoundly changing lives and helping people live longer with her new brand, AlkaMiracle, Living Water.

@aiechia_ (on IG)

@Aiechia Davis (on Facebook)

Vyda Azul, YouTube Guru

This amazing woman has been in my life for about 2 years now. We met each other towards the end of 2019, I believe. We were in a manifesting group that taught the practices of Law of Attraction. We hit it off instantly. We grew into each other daily by texting, calling and just being that person that will tell you, "ok sis, not today" or "you had your moment of being mad, angry or sad, time to brush it off." While we were there for each other in that way, we also watched our lives change drastically right before our eyes. Both of us have grown and are not where we were when we met. I said all of that to say that I am grateful for her being in my life, even if we do not talk everyday like we used to; when we do talk, we know what time it is.

Life's Magical Journey

https://www.youtube.com/channel/UCGxqbSerzarloGmWk7OUfcA

Stephanie Hawkins, My Best Friend

This amazing woman has been in my life since 2013, yeah, that is a long time. I was ending a marriage, in school etc. at that time. We both were in an algebra class together that we did not want to be in. I think I reached out and asked if any of us wanted to help each other, and she responded. Since then, we have been like glue. We have been through a lot together and we are both there to help pick the other up. She has been my backbone when no one was. I am so grateful to have her in my life and can't wait to meet her in person. Yeah, we've been lifelong Facebook friends, lol.

Love you!

Dr. Tonya Blackmon, Business Developer & Queen of Grants

Me and Dr. Tonya have known each other for almost 1-2 years now. We met through our mutual friend Minister now Dr. Nakita Davis; a collaborative book named Bossmoms: You Can Have It All with Christ. I do not remember exactly, but she ended up being a speaker at my Let us Change Together Event, 2020. Since then, she has been my coach in business. She is wayyyyyy more than that, let me tell you, but without spilling the beans, let us just say I'm honored and blessed to have this amazing woman of God in my life. I choose to honor her because of the impact she has on my life in unexplainable ways.

www.drtonyab.com

Tenesa Mobley, Founder of Power of You

This is my sissssss of sisses. I really love her. We met and spoke through the connection of Dr. Tonya. Since the time, we worked together, a business relationship turned personal. She has been there for me, and she also goes out of her way to help anyone. This amazing queen is quick to tell what is and what it is not, and I love her more for that. I can honestly say she is another woman who has my back.

www.thepowerofyouga.com

Minister Nakita Davis, Owner of Jesus Coffee and Prayer

I could not do a collaborative book without honoring her. Yes, I started my children's books and published them on my own but the supernatural blessings started with being in hers. She put together Bossmoms: You Can Have It All with Christ, published it and everything turned around for me. I have been able to connect with amazing women through her just by being in the book. Even after months passed, Bam! December of 2020, she blessed all her authors by landing us on Billboard in Atlanta, Ga. This woman has been such a blessing to me in many ways regarding business and I am grateful to God for the connection.

www.jesuscoffeeandprayer.com

Evonn Firms, Evangelist and Ghostwriter

I also met Mrs. Evonn through Minister Nakita. Since knowing and communicating with her, she has also blessed my life. Time after time, being a small business owner, we want people to share, like, comment on our posts, right? Well, this awesome woman right here, does it without me expecting it every time. I genuinely appreciate her support and I do not think she knows how much I do. It means a lot to see her sharing my posts and supporting me the ways she does. Support is not always about money; it is the smallest things that matter. Thank you from the bottom of my heart.

https://www.facebook.com/InspiredbyEonly

Tina Ramsay, Owner of The Tina Ramsay Show

I am honored to be honoring this amazing woman. Since connecting with her, she has placed a blessing upon me I cannot explain or mention. I will say that I deeply appreciate her for everything she does and the words she places in my heart when we talk. In business, it is unexplainable as to how she blesses me, and I am so grateful for her. Me and Mrs. Tina must keep our conversations short because we will talk for hours, lol. You're an amazing woman and I thank you.

www.coachtinaramsay.com

TeKeisha Wade, Owner of Open Arms Connection LLC

We were both co-authors in the Bossmoms: You Can Have It All with Christ. When we connected, we connected. Things I cannot mention of course, but let me say, she has also been a blessing to me. We feed each other spiritually. We have counseled each other in situations we were in and needed each other. I am grateful for her spirit. She has this small presence about her, but the Holy Spirit speaks loudly through her, and in that, speaks volumes. I am so grateful to see how much she has grown since we met, and she is continuing to grow daily. There is more to her than what meets the eye.

www.openarmsconnection.com

Martika Jackson, Owner of Sheabutter Empowerment

We met in 2020 in a group we were in. She is so bubbly, and I love that about her. We have talked so many times since then and sometimes it is late at night when we do. I am so grateful for the connection we have because I have also watched her grow since we met. She has been there for me also on personal levels and I to her. She has a big footprint when she steps out and make a lot of noise positively in her community and I'm so proud of her. Keep it up mamas; you got this!

www.sheabutterempowerment.com

Destiny Kingcannon, Owner of Destiny Inspired LLC

This awesome queen is also my coach. I am beyond grateful for how she has blessed me when and after I attended her Sis Speak Up Cohort in February 2021. Her words come packed with God's spirit in a way that meets you on the level you're on. While she gets you to realize how you are, she helps build your confidence to do things you didn't want to do or you thought you couldn't do. I specifically chose to honor her to let her know how great she is in my life. If you are not ready, she is going to help you be ready when she gets done with you, lol. She brings out the spots in you that were hidden.

www.destinyinspire.com

Here are some Manifesting Scriptures.

1 Corinthians 12:7

To each is given the manifestation of the Spirit for the common good.

Ephesians 3:20

Now to him who is able to do far more abundantly than all that we ask or think, according to the power at work within us.

1 Corinthians 3:13

Each one's work will become manifest, for the Day will disclose it, because it will be revealed by fire, and the fire will test what sort of work each one has done.

1 Timothy 3:16

Great indeed, we confess, is the mystery of godliness: He was manifested in the flesh, vindicated by the Spirit, seen by angels, proclaimed among the nations, believed on in the world, taken up in glory.

Luke 8:17

"For nothing is hidden that will not be made manifest, nor is anything secret that will not be known and come to light."

Here are some Faith Scriptures

Matthew 21:22 ESV

And whatever you ask in prayer, you will receive, if you have faith."

Hebrews 11:6 ESV

And without faith, it is impossible to please him, for whoever would draw near to God must believe that he exists and that he rewards those who seek him.

Romans 10:17 ESV

So faith comes from hearing, and hearing through the word of Christ.

Hebrews 11:1 ESV

Now faith is the assurance of things hoped for, the conviction of things not seen.

Mark 11:22-24 ESV

And Jesus answered them, "Have faith in God. Truly, I say to you, whoever says to this mountain, 'Be taken up and thrown into the sea,' and does not doubt in his heart, but believes that what he says will come to pass, it will be done for him.

Therefore I tell you, whatever you ask in prayer, believe that you have received it, and it will be yours.

Ephesians 2:8-9 ESV

For by grace you have been saved through faith. And this is not your own doing; it is the gift of God, not a result of works, so that no one may boast.

James 2:19 ESV

You believe that God is one; you do well. Even the demons believe—and shudder!

Proverbs 3:5-6 ESV

Trust in the Lord with all your heart, and do not lean on your own understanding. In all your ways acknowledge him, and he will make straight your paths.

2 Corinthians 5:7 ESV

For we walk by faith, not by sight.

Luke 1:37 ESV

For nothing will be impossible with God."

Ephesians 2:8 ESV

For by grace you have been saved through faith. And this is not your own doing; it is the gift of God,

1 Corinthians 2:5 ESV

That your faith might not rest in the wisdom of men but in the power of God.

John 3:16 ESV

"For God so loved the world, that he gave his only Son, that whoever believes in him should not perish but have eternal life.

Hebrews 11:1-13:25

Now faith is the assurance of things hoped for, the conviction of things not seen. For by it the people of old received their commendation. By faith we understand that the universe was created by the word of God, so that what is seen was not made out of things that are visible. By faith Abel offered to God a more acceptable sacrifice than Cain, through which he was commended as righteous, God commending him by accepting his gifts. And through his faith, though he died, he still speaks. By faith Enoch was taken up so that he should not see death, and he was not found, because God had taken him. Now before he was taken he was commended as having pleased God. ...

Philippians 4:13 ESV

I can do all things through him who strengthens me.

James 2:14-26 ESV

What good is it, my brothers, if someone says he has faith but does not have works? Can that faith save him? If a brother or sister is poorly clothed and lacking in daily food, and one of you says to them, "Go in peace, be warmed and filled," without giving them the things needed for the body, what good is that? So also faith by itself, if it does not have works, is dead. But someone will say, "You have faith and I have works." Show me your faith apart from your works, and I will show you my faith by my works. ...

James 1:5-8 ESV

If any of you lacks wisdom, let him ask God, who gives generously to all without reproach, and it will be given him. But let him ask in faith, with no doubting, for the one who doubts is like a wave of the sea that is driven and tossed by the wind. For that person must not suppose that he will receive anything from the Lord; he is a double-minded man, unstable in all his ways.

James 2:24 ESV

You see that a person is justified by works and not by faith alone.

Mark 9:23 ESV

And Jesus said to him, "If you can!' All things are possible for one who believes."

Luke 17:5 ESV

The apostles said to the Lord, "Increase our faith!"

Matthew 17:20 ESV

He said to them, "Because of your little faith. For truly, I say to you, if you have faith like a grain of mustard seed, you will say to this mountain, 'Move from here to there,' and it will move, and nothing will be impossible for you."

Matthew 21:21-22 ESV

And Jesus answered them, "Truly, I say to you, if you have faith and do not doubt, you will not only do what has been done to the fig tree, but even if you say to this mountain, 'Be taken up and thrown into the sea,' it will happen. And whatever you ask in prayer, you will receive, if you have faith."

Galatians 2:20 ESV

I have been crucified with Christ. It is no longer I who live, but Christ who lives in me. And the life I now live in the flesh I live by faith in the Son of God, who loved me and gave himself for me.

Hebrews 11:1-40 ESV

Now faith is the assurance of things hoped for, the conviction of things not seen. For by it the people of old received their commendation. By faith we understand that the universe was created by the word of God, so that what is seen was not made out of things that are visible. By faith Abel offered to God a more acceptable sacrifice than Cain, through which he was commended as righteous, God commending him by accepting his gifts. And through his faith, though he died, he still speaks. By faith Enoch was taken up so that he should not see death, and he was not found because God had taken him. Now before he was taken he was commended as having pleased God. ...

2 Timothy 4:7 ESV

I have fought the good fight, I have finished the race, I have kept the faith.

1 Corinthians 13:13 ESV

So now faith, hope, and love abide, these three; but the greatest of these is love.

1 John 5:4 ESV

For everyone who has been born of God overcomes the world. And this is the victory that has overcome the world—our faith.

Romans 12:3 ESV

For by the grace given to me I say to everyone among you not to think of himself more highly than he ought to think, but to think with sober judgment, each according to the measure of faith that God has assigned.

Psalm 46:10 ESV

"Be still, and know that I am God. I will be exalted among the nations, I will be exalted in the earth!"

1 Corinthians 16:13 ESV

Be watchful, stand firm in the faith, act like men, be strong.

Mark 10:52 ESV

And Jesus said to him, "Go your way; your faith has made you well." And immediately he recovered his sight and followed him on the way.

Romans 15:13 ESV

May the God of hope fill you with all joy and peace in believing, so that by the power of the Holy Spirit you may abound in hope.

Galatians 2:16 ESV

Yet we know that a person is not justified by works of the law but through faith in Jesus Christ, so we also have believed in Christ Jesus, in order to be justified by faith in Christ and not by works of the law, because by works of the law no one will be justified.

Ephesians 6:16 ESV

In all circumstances take up the shield of faith, with which you can extinguish all the flaming darts of the evil one;

Romans 1:17 ESV

For in it the righteousness of God is revealed from faith for faith, as it is written, "The righteous shall live by faith."

Romans 10:9 ESV

Because, if you confess with your mouth that Jesus is Lord and believe in your heart that God raised him from the dead, you will be saved.

Matthew 21:21 ESV

And Jesus answered them, "Truly, I say to you, if you have faith and do not doubt, you will not only do what has been done to the fig tree, but even if you say to this mountain, 'Be taken up and thrown into the sea,' it will happen.

John 8:24 ESV

I told you that you would die in your sins, for unless you believe that I am he you will die in your sins."

Hebrews 11:7 ESV

By faith Noah, being warned by God concerning events as yet unseen, in reverent fear constructed an ark for the saving of his household. By this he condemned the world and became an heir of the righteousness that comes by faith.

Mark 11:24 ESV

Therefore I tell you, whatever you ask in prayer, believe that you have received it, and it will be yours.

Mark 16:16 ESV

Whoever believes and is baptized will be saved, but whoever does not believe will be condemned.

James 1:6 ESV

But let him ask in faith, with no doubting, for the one who doubts is like a wave of the sea that is driven and tossed by the wind.

James 1:3 ESV

For you know that the testing of your faith produces steadfastness.

James 2:17 ESV

So also faith by itself, if it does not have works, is dead.

Habakkuk 2:4 ESV

"Behold, his soul is puffed up; it is not upright within him, but the righteous shall live by his faith.

John 6:35 ESV

Jesus said to them, "I am the bread of life; whoever comes to me shall not hunger, and whoever believes in me shall never thirst.

John 3:36 ESV

Whoever believes in the Son has eternal life; whoever does not obey the Son shall not see life, but the wrath of God remains on him.

Hebrews 12:2 ESV

Looking to Jesus, the founder and perfecter of our faith, who for the joy that was set before him endured the cross, despising the shame, and is seated at the right hand of the throne of God.

1 Corinthians 13:2 ESV

And if I have prophetic powers, and understand all mysteries and all knowledge, and if I have all faith, so as to remove mountains, but have not love, I am nothing.

1 Timothy 6:12 ESV

Fight the good fight of the faith. Take hold of the eternal life to which you were called and about which you made the good confession in the presence of many witnesses.

Matthew 15:28 ESV

Then Jesus answered her, "O woman, great is your faith! Be it done for you as you desire." And her daughter was healed instantly.

Luke 18:27 ESV

But he said, "What is impossible with men is possible with God."

Proverbs 3:5 ESV

Trust in the Lord with all your heart, and do not lean on your own understanding.

John 11:25-26 ESV

Jesus said to her, "I am the resurrection and the life. Whoever believes in me, though he die, yet shall he live, and everyone who lives and believes in me shall never die. Do you believe this?"

Romans 4:20-21 ESV

No distrust made him waver concerning the promise of God, but he grew strong in his faith as he gave glory to God, fully convinced that God was able to do what he had promised.

Psalm 23:1-6 ESV

A Psalm of David. The Lord is my shepherd; I shall not want. He makes me lie down in green pastures. He leads me beside still waters. He restores my soul. He leads me in paths of righteousness for his name's sake. Even though I walk through the valley of the shadow of death, I will fear no evil, for you are with me; your rod and your staff, they comfort me. You prepare a table before me in the presence of my enemies; you anoint my head with oil; my cup overflows. ...

John 7:38 ESV

Whoever believes in me, as the Scripture has said, 'Out of his heart will flow rivers of living water.'"

Romans 14:1 ESV

As for the one who is weak in faith, welcome him, but not to quarrel over opinions.

1 Corinthians 10:13 ESV

No temptation has overtaken you that is not common to man. God is faithful, and he will not let you be tempted beyond your ability, but with the temptation he will also provide the way of escape, that you may be able to endure it.

Mark 11:22 ESV

And Jesus answered them, "Have faith in God.

1 Peter 3:15 ESV

But in your hearts honor Christ the Lord as holy, always being prepared to make a defense to anyone who asks you for a reason for the hope that is in you; yet do it with gentleness and respect,

Ephesians 3:16-17 ESV

That according to the riches of his glory he may grant you to be strengthened with power through his Spirit in your inner being, so that Christ may dwell in your hearts through faith—that you, being rooted and grounded in love,

Hebrews 11:11 ESV

Romans 4:20-21 ESV

No distrust made him waver concerning the promise of God, but he grew strong in his faith as he gave glory to God, fully convinced that God was able to do what he had promised.

Psalm 23:1-6 ESV

A Psalm of David. The Lord is my shepherd; I shall not want. He makes me lie down in green pastures. He leads me beside still waters. He restores my soul. He leads me in paths of righteousness for his name's sake. Even though I walk through the valley of the shadow of death, I will fear no evil, for you are with me; your rod and your staff, they comfort me. You prepare a table before me in the presence of my enemies; you anoint my head with oil; my cup overflows. ...

John 7:38 ESV

Whoever believes in me, as the Scripture has said, 'Out of his heart will flow rivers of living water.'"

Romans 14:1 ESV

As for the one who is weak in faith, welcome him, but not to quarrel over opinions.

1 Corinthians 10:13 ESV

No temptation has overtaken you that is not common to man. God is faithful, and he will not let you be tempted beyond your ability, but with the temptation he will also provide the way of escape, that you may be able to endure it.

Mark 11:22 ESV

And Jesus answered them, "Have faith in God.

1 Peter 3:15 ESV

But in your hearts honor Christ the Lord as holy, always being prepared to make a defense to anyone who asks you for a reason for the hope that is in you; yet do it with gentleness and respect,

Ephesians 3:16-17 ESV

That according to the riches of his glory he may grant you to be strengthened with power through his Spirit in your inner being, so that Christ may dwell in your hearts through faith—that you, being rooted and grounded in love,

Hebrews 11:11 ESV

By faith Sarah herself received power to conceive, even when she was past the age, since she considered him faithful who had promised.

Romans 1:16-17 ESV

For I am not ashamed of the gospel, for it is the power of God for salvation to everyone who believes, to the Jew first and also to the Greek. For in it the righteousness of God is revealed from faith for faith, as it is written, "The righteous shall live by faith."

1 Peter 1:8-9 ESV

Though you have not seen him, you love him. Though you do not now see him, you believe in him and rejoice with joy that is inexpressible and filled with glory, obtaining the outcome of your faith, the salvation of your souls.

1 Peter 1:7 ESV

So that the tested genuineness of your faith—more precious than gold that perishes though it is tested by fire—may be found to result in praise and glory and honor at the revelation of Jesus Christ.

Galatians 5:22 ESV

But the fruit of the Spirit is love, joy, peace, patience, kindness, goodness, faithfulness,

John 1:1 ESV

In the beginning was the Word, and the Word was with God, and the Word was God.

1 Timothy 6:11 ESV

But as for you, O man of God, flee these things. Pursue righteousness, godliness, faith, love, steadfastness, gentleness.

Matthew 6:24 ESV

"No one can serve two masters, for either he will hate the one and love the other, or he will be devoted to the one and despise the other. You cannot serve God and money.

Romans 10:10 ESV

For with the heart one believes and is justified, and with the mouth one confesses and is saved.

John 1:12 ESV

But to all who did receive him, who believed in his name, he gave the right to become children of God,

James 2:18 ESV

But someone will say, "You have faith and I have works." Show me your faith apart from your works, and I will show you my faith by my works.

Jeremiah 29:11 ESV

For I know the plans I have for you, declares the Lord, plans for welfare and not for evil, to give you a future and a hope.

Proverbs 3:6 ESV

In all your ways acknowledge him, and he will make straight your paths.

John 11:40 ESV

Jesus said to her, "Did I not tell you that if you believed you would see the glory of God?"

1 John 5:1 ESV

Everyone who believes that Jesus is the Christ has been born of God, and everyone who loves the Father loves whoever has been born of him.

Matthew 9:22 ESV

Jesus turned, and seeing her he said, "Take heart, daughter; your faith has made you well." And instantly the woman was made well.

Luke 17:6 ESV

And the Lord said, "If you had faith like a grain of mustard seed, you could say to this mulberry tree, 'Be uprooted and planted in the sea,' and it would obey you.

2 Corinthians 5:6-7 ESV

So we are always of good courage. We know that while we are at home in the body we are away from the Lord, for we walk by faith, not by sight.

Galatians 5:6 ESV

For in Christ Jesus neither circumcision nor uncircumcision counts for anything, but only faith working through love.

Hebrews 10:38 ESV

But my righteous one shall live by faith, and if he shrinks back, my soul has no pleasure in him."

Joshua 1:9 ESV

Have I not commanded you? Be strong and courageous. Do not be frightened, and do not be dismayed, for the Lord your God is with you wherever you go."

Romans 14:23 ESV

But whoever has doubts is condemned if he eats, because the eating is not from faith. For whatever does not proceed from faith is sin.

Philippians 4:19 ESV

And my God will supply every need of yours according to his riches in glory in Christ Jesus.

1 Thessalonians 1:3 ESV

Remembering before our God and Father your work of faith and labor of love and steadfastness of hope in our Lord Jesus Christ.

John 6:47 ESV

Truly, truly, I say to you, whoever believes has eternal life.

Galatians 3:26 ESV

For in Christ Jesus you are all sons of God, through faith.

Luke 7:50 ESV

And he said to the woman, "Your faith has saved you; go in peace."

Romans 5:1 ESV

Therefore, since we have been justified by faith, we have peace with God through our Lord Jesus Christ.

Romans 5:1-5 ESV

Therefore, since we have been justified by faith, we have peace with God through our Lord Jesus Christ. Through him we have also obtained access by faith into this grace in which we stand, and we rejoice in hope of the glory of God. More than that, we rejoice in our sufferings, knowing that suffering produces endurance, and endurance produces character, and character produces hope, and hope does not put us to shame, because God's love has been poured into our hearts through the Holy Spirit who has been given to us.

Romans 8:28 ESV

And we know that for those who love God all things work together for good, for those who are called according to his purpose.

John 20:31 ESV

But these are written so that you may believe that Jesus is the Christ, the Son of God, and that by believing you may have life in his name.

Isaiah 40:31 ESV

But they who wait for the Lord shall renew their strength; they shall mount up with wings like eagles; they shall run and not be weary; they shall walk and not faint.

1 John 5:13 ESV

I write these things to you who believe in the name of the Son of God that you may know that you have eternal life.

1 Timothy 1:19 ESV

Holding faith and a good conscience. By rejecting this, some have made shipwreck of their faith,

Romans 8:24-25 ESV

For in this hope we were saved. Now hope that is seen is not hope. For who hopes for what he sees? But if we hope for what we do not see, we wait for it with patience.

www.ingramcontent.com/pod-product-compliance
Lightning Source LLC
Chambersburg PA
CBHW080747300426
44114CB00019B/2666